Prais

An Unbreakable Spirit

An Unbreakable Spirit is a story of the hope, redemption, and strength that are found only in the peace and comfort of God. The author's son, Clint, lives life the only way he knows how. He is kind, genuine, and authentic. He becomes a role model through this journey. What unfolds will captivate your inner core with laughter and tears. Kindness and forgiveness are illustrated throughout the story.

If you are searching for a way to make it through another day, you have found a great example in the life of the author and her family. The book is an honest portrayal of struggles with relationships, illness, and forgiveness. So much loss is shared in this story, and yet an unbreakable spirit shines through.

—Suzanne Ray, LICSW.

***

I could not stop reading… a heartfelt emotional journey that shows love, loss, despair, and triumph. An Unbreakable spirit illustrates the love from a parent to her child.

—Maggie Thrower, Director, Arab, Al. Senior Center.

***

If you have been through struggles, this story will help you realize that you are never alone. An Unbreakable Spirit illustrates the faithfulness of the Lord and the realization that there is always hope, no matter what life throws at you.

I could not put this book down because I wanted to know what happened next. I felt like I was living the story with the author. I laughed, cried, and was inspired throughout her journey.

—Wendy Pemberton, Reliability Engineer.

***

I really enjoyed reading this book. I found it easy to follow and the story flowed very well. It is hard to put down. I kept telling myself, "I will read just one more chapter and then put it down." I did this through fourteen chapters.

An Unbreakable Spirit hit almost every emotion—joy, sadness, anger, and thankfulness. But most of all, I found it extremely inspiring. No matter the situation, this family just keeps on pushing through. In a nutshell, I would give this book 5 out of 5 stars!

—**Barry Plunkett**, Business Owner.

***

In her reflections on the circumstances of the past decade of her life, the author reminds us of the incredible power of love, faith, and prayer. She weaves a beautiful, often humorous, and inspirational story full of life lessons. Despite many tragedies, the author manages to find triumph in the little things that matter the most. Once, overcome by grief and anger, she finds refuge in her faith, as well as a new outlook on life.

This is a fantastic, personal story. The reader will be left reflecting on their own life and circumstances and will learn not to take any moment for granted. This is a must read!

—**Stephanie Spano**, U.S. Army, LTC (Ret.), Thirty-One Gifts Independent Director.

***

Very rarely do I begin a book and read all the way to chapter 22 in a single day! This book was easy to read and very interesting. At the end of every chapter, I had to read the next one because I was eager to find out what happened next. Even though I "knew" most of these events, reading about them gave me the feeling of "living" the journey with the family. It was very inspirational and gave me encouragement and comfort in knowing that people can overcome even the most difficult of circumstances! Definitely 5 stars!!

—**Angela Plunkett,** Chief Administrative Officer.

An Unbreakable Spirit

Paula Bullock Mecomber

Published by KHARIS PUBLISHING, imprint of KHARIS MEDIA LLC.

Copyright © 2021 Paula Bullock Mecomber

ISBN-13: 978-1-63746-066-5

ISBN-10: 1-63746-066-X

Library of Congress Control Number: 2021938222

All Scripture quotations, unless otherwise indicated, are taken from the Holy Bible, New Revised Standard Version ®, RSV®. Copyright ©1973, 1978, 1984, 2011 by Biblical, Inc.™ Used by permission.

All KHARIS PUBLISHING products are available at special quantity discounts for bulk purchase for sales promotions, premiums, fund-raising, and educational needs. For details, contact:

Kharis Media LLC
Tel: 1-479-599-8657
support@kharispublishing.com
www.kharispublishing.com

CONTENTS

CHAPTER 1

Some friends and I were at a dance club in Huntsville when Travis came and asked me to dance. The year was 1987. I was nineteen and he was twenty-two. He was buff, with big blue eyes and a beautiful smile. He was a guy's guy—you know, the type that is very masculine and confident. As I found out, he was originally from Texas and had just gotten out of the Army. I remember being shocked that someone so handsome was asking me to dance. We danced the night away and the next day he came and picked me up for lunch. We were inseparable from that point on.

By the spring of 1988, we were married. The first couple of years were carefree. Looking back, we were just kids really. We rented a house and worked hard during the day and partied and frolicked at night. My parents thought that I was too young to be married. After some time, though, they realized that I was happy and came to accept Travis as a son. In those days, we did not have much. Travis worked at a flooring retail store and I worked at a rental car company. We shared a car and would ride together to work each day.

In the summer of 1989, Travis was offered a job selling insurance in Albertville, Alabama. The offer came with the possibility of more money. It was a career type job. It also put us closer to my parents who lived in Guntersville. We moved. The insurance job required a lot of hours. Building up a route and client base was difficult in the beginning. Since we only had one car, I stayed home while Travis worked. Those days were very isolating and lonely. The feeling of being trapped swept over me. But through it all, I tried to remain positive and supportive. In his line of work, Travis was required to attend many after-hour events. Some included spouses and some did not. At the ones that I attended, I started observing changes in my husband. I was always fine with being a little inconspicuous but not Travis; he was a natural born salesman, always the life of every event. I felt like we were growing apart.

Sometime in 1989, I suggested that we try to have a baby. I was twenty-one at this point, and thought I was ready. I kept thinking that my mom started having children at twenty. My grandmother before her had started her family at eighteen. I now realize I had no internal clock ticking. I was just trying to fill the void of being home all day alone and was trying to bring me and Travis closer together. A baby solidifies these bonds, right?

It did not take long for me to get pregnant. I found out I was expecting a baby due early in the spring. The next months were spent getting a nursery ready, planning baby showers, and ballooning out. I gained over seventy pounds during those nine months. A week before my due date, I developed a migraine like no other headache I had ever experienced. I went to the hospital and my blood pressure was sky-high. They started watching me very closely. At the same time, Travis was still trying to build his career. A lot of nights, he would go to after-hour events and not arrive back home until bedtime.

At 11:56pm on March 16, 1990, Clinton Hollis Williams was born. I was so excited about the birth of my son. But I was also scared to death. What if I was not a good mom? Or what if something happened to him while on my watch? How would I know what he needed while he was so small and did not communicate except for crying? Apart from a few babysitting jobs, I had never been responsible for a child, especially a newborn, and, as I found out, babies do not come with instructions.

Since Clint was born so late in the evening, the hospital just gave me a short time with him and then he was off to the nursery for his check-up. My family had been at the hospital all day; every one of them was exhausted. So, when the nurse took Clint for the evening, they decided to go home to sleep and return the following morning.

I hardly slept a wink that night. It is amazing what giving birth does—it changes you instantly. I could not stop thinking: "Wow, I am a mom now."

My family had not returned yet by 6:00am the next morning when the nurse brought Clint to me along with some diapers, bottles, and cloths which I later found out were for burping. She said, "Here's your little boy."

As she turned to leave the room, panic set in, and I yelled out: "Wait, what am I supposed to do?"

The nurse was looking at me like I was an idiot. I collected my thoughts and started again: "How much of this bottle do I need to give him before he will need to burp?"

With that, she gave me very brief instructions and promptly left the room.

And there the journey began. Babies are awesome, frustrating, incredible, fun, and, at times, difficult. Yet, I believe that no greater joy exists than giving birth to a child of your own. The feeling of knowing that a little person is so dependent on you, loyal to you, and unconditionally in love with you, is indescribable. But even stronger is the realization that there is now someone who means more to you than your own life does. Someone who motivates you to do whatever it takes to keep them healthy, happy, and safe. There is no bond stronger than that of a mother with her children.

I looked down at the sweetest face I had ever seen.

I muttered, "Well, kid, looks like it is just you and me. I don't know a lot about this yet, but bear with me and we will figure it all out together."

I gave him his bottle and just stared at him. He was the prettiest baby I had ever seen. He weighed almost eleven pounds at birth and had the most perfectly shaped round face, alert eyes, and the softest skin. He was not scrawny looking like some newborns are, but more like a little doll. As far as I was concerned, he was perfect.

I gave him about half of his bottle, and he started squirming. I put him up on my shoulder and he let out the biggest burp and then went fast asleep right there in my arms, totally at peace. He obviously had more confidence in me than I did. And I realized we had in fact figured it out. Unbeknownst to me, that would only be the beginning of the struggles we would have to face together.

When we got home, things were seemingly fine for a while. But when Clint turned nine months old, I realized that something was wrong. Clint was still not sitting up by himself. I took him to his pediatrician, and he agreed that Clint was not developing at a normal pace. That initial consultation brought another eighteen months of testing, trips to the Children's hospital, MRI's, and visits to a bunch of different specialists.

When Clint was two years old, the doctor finally diagnosed him. The doctor, a female with the bedside manner of a rock, came into the room, and, offering no small talk, no lead in, she gave me no time to prepare for what she was about to say. She just walked into the room, looked briskly at her files, cleared her throat, and said, "Your son is severely mentally retarded, and will probably never walk or talk. The best thing you can do is just take him home and love him. There is nothing more that we can do for him."

With that she closed her file folder and left the room. I was in shock, heartbroken, angry, and hurt. How dare she be so uncaring? At the same time, I questioned her diagnosis. I was sure that there was something wrong with my son; after all, I was the one who had pointed it out to the pediatrician. And while I was not a doctor, only a mother, I was with my child every day. I also knew that there was more going on than she was willing to consider. Clint and I had our own communication, He understood things. She could not possibly be right!

Initially after the diagnosis, I went through periods of feeling sorry for myself and of feeling sorry for Clint as well. I had feelings of anger, helplessness, and guilt. You can name an emotion and I probably felt it. Shortly thereafter, I decided that I needed to be more informed and handle Clint's diagnosis head on. I still did not believe it, but I was determined to do all that I could do to afford him the best life he could have.

One afternoon I called a Medical Data Information Center (this was before the days of the internet, WEB MD, or the likes). The Center was funded by the hospital and the phones were manned by retired doctors and nurses. They had information and pamphlets on almost every disease or condition, and, upon request, would send them to you. The decision to call wound up being a good one. I spoke with a retired doctor. The interaction imparted knowledge to me in ways I cannot really explain. He sent me a wealth of information about retardation and about the importance of early intervention in children with developmental delays.

The most important thing, though, was something that he said— "Don't get caught up on labels; doctors don't always have all the answers and sometimes they are simply wrong. But the one thing I can tell you is that retardation is just a word that means slowed, and everyone is retarded or slowed in some way or another; some people have mental limitations, some physical, like arthritis or heart disease, etc., but everyone has some sort of slowed or retarded ability."

That advice really put things into perspective. Everyone has limitations, right? Some are more easily overcome than others, but we all have limitations nonetheless.

After that phone call, I made a conscious effort to never get stuck on any label nor use one as an excuse to make Clint believe there was something he could not do, at least not until he tried. I also decided that from that point on, I would do all that I could to be proactive. If there was anything that I could do to help Clint or improve the quality of his life, I made it my mission to do so. I also realized that there would be no time for pity for him or myself; life is too short for that nonsense.

Another profound thing that made an impact on my thinking at the time was something that my Aunt Flora told me. Aunt Flora was a retired schoolteacher, and she was one of the most insightful people I ever knew. She was very smart, sweet, and soft-spoken. After Clint was diagnosed, she said to me, "Clint is lucky to have you as his mother because God always places the right children with the right parent. God chose you to have this special child because he knew that with you Clint would learn a lot and would always be loved."

Those words have stuck with me for decades. *God chose you to have this special child.* What I came to realize is what a true blessing that choosing was. I was the lucky one. I also came to know that while Clint may have learned from me throughout the years, I was the one who got the biggest lessons. Clint always seemed to teach me more. In fact, he was probably my best teacher on life lessons, the ones dealing with humanity, kindness, perseverance, and patience.

One of the first proactive things that I did was to find Clint another doctor. Clint had been tugging at his ears for years. I had mentioned it to the specialist but they refused to check them. They would tell me that I was grasping at straws and that I just needed to accept their diagnosis and move on. I found a doctor who had just started his own practice. For the first appointment, I left Clint with my mom and went alone and just paid for an hour of his time, to bring him up to speed on what had happened to that point, and to let him know what I would expect of Clint's new doctor. That was empowering. I wanted someone who was going to be on "team Clint," and would listen to my concerns. I also told him about Clint pulling on his ears. And while I did not think that was the entire source of Clint's delays, I did believe that there was something going on with them that warranted investigation. He agreed.

He told me it only took a few minutes to do a tympanogram an ear test that checks the pressure in the ear. "That would quickly rule out or confirm ear problems."

I booked an appointment for Clint. When the results came back, we were all shocked to find that his ears were both full of fluid and had been for a while. The doctor told me that with all the fluid in his ears, all Clint was hearing were muffled sounds. It was the equivalent of hearing and trying to learn to talk while being underwater. We immediately scheduled surgery to have drainage tubes put into his ears. He was about two and half at the time.

Within days of the tubes being put in his ears, Clint started babbling and learning words. The transformation was amazing. But there was a lot of lost time. Clint had some difficulty with learning blended sound words like his own name. He could not say the Cl sound, so Clint became Dut. For two years after, Clint would tell everyone that his name was Dut. In fact, he kind of developed his own language; he would say the same words for the same things consistently. He understood what he was communicating.

It was fun to watch him develop. He was still struggling to catch up with the "milestones," but he was walking and talking and he potty trained. His dad and I hired a speech therapist. She worked with him for a couple of years and by the time Clint started school, he was talking up a storm.

On the home front, things were not going so well. Working with Clint and being a stay-at-home mom consumed my time. As years went by, Travis continued to climb the ladder at the insurance company and the two of us both grew up. The only problem was that we did not grow in the same direction; we grew apart. Clint became my purpose in life. Travis, on the other hand, idealized the perfect home; perfect clothes, perfect vacations, that sort of thing. In all honesty, there were days when I barely showered. He tried to convince me to go and get my nails done, hair done. He would buy me nice outfits, and, honestly, I tried to embrace that lifestyle but it just wasn't me.

Late in 1996, I got a phone call from another agent who worked with Travis. A woman named Lisa. I had met her several times before. She turned out to have the persona of the woman that Travis was trying to turn me into, the perfect picture of put-togetherness. She had perfectly coifed nails and hair, perfume, and cleavage. She called to inform me that she and Travis had been having an affair, and that her husband had found out and was divorcing her. She believed that Travis was going to leave me, too, and be with her. After her husband had filed for divorce, she realized that Travis was not moving toward divorce. She said that she just felt I should know.

Let us be honest, she was not telling me because she cared about me. She was hurt and lashing out at Travis. I however had no idea about their affair. Her phone call left me with a punch to the gut. All those late nights did not always include work as he had told me. I was crushed.

In April of 1997, Travis and I separated and subsequently divorced. This was hard on Clint. Because of his disabilities, structure and routine were important. Clint and I moved in with my parents for a couple of months and then into an apartment. The first couple of years were difficult for us both, dealing with all the changes, moving, financial struggles, and Clint going back and forth between my house and his dad's house took a toll. Once again though, Clint and I worked through all those changes together. I finally got on my feet, landed a great job with The Tennessee Valley Authority (TVA), and, in 1999, bought my own house. Clint and I were on the right track again.

During that time, my mom and dad were also helpful. Clint was their only grandchild. They loved him so much and were always so supportive. But that relationship became more important after the divorce, when I went back to work; I can honestly say that I could not have done life at that time without them. They were so instrumental in Clint's development too. My mom was just the perfect grandmother. My dad and Clint were buddies. My dad spent a lot of time with Clint, reading, fishing, shooting a BB gun, telling corny jokes, and talking. This relationship would prove to be one of the most important in Clint's life. Clint initially called my dad papaw, but one day he misspoke and accidently called him pa-pooh. They got so tickled and from that point on, my dad became pa-pooh to everyone.

There were also struggles for Clint when he started school. During his kindergarten years, instead of grades, his teacher drew happy faces on the student's papers to show her approval of their work. With Clint, she always put frowny faces because she told him that his work was not as good as the other kids. He was discouraged and told me that he was trying as hard as he could. It broke my heart.

Shortly after that, the school started doing their own testing on Clint. They determined that his IQ was around 60, putting him in the category of mildly to moderately mentally retarded. He was put into special education classes. He also was given occupational therapy and continued with speech therapy. He did well. Clint also had some mainstream classes, with the help of an aide, for the purpose of the social interaction. In those classes, he took tests and did the same assignments as his mainstream classmates, but his grades were modified. We went through years of Independent Educational Plan (IEP) meetings and further testing, but without much change in his diagnosis.

During the next few years, Clint thrived in many areas of his life but continued to really struggle in others. It was puzzling to watch him learn. With some things, he just did not get it, things like addition and subtraction, or riding a bicycle, or conversational social cues. He would sometimes talk about random things that interested him without regard to what other conversations were going on around him. He also struggled with basic skills like how many quarters were in a dollar or being able to follow basic multi-stepped directions.

But with other things his brain was amazing. And while his comprehension was not strong, he did learn to read and to write, to tie his shoes, and to do tricks with a yo-yo. He practiced and practiced until he mastered it. He loved music and music trivia, video games, and he loved to look up facts on the computer about people and things that interested him. At one point he developed an interest in martial arts, specifically Bruce Lee. Clint looked up all the information about Bruce Lee that he could find. He would gladly recite to us and anyone else how tall Bruce Lee was, where he was born, the names of his movies, how he died, and so on. He loved reading the World Book of Records. He also developed quite a sense of humor. Clean but corny humor. I think he got that from my dad. He would share a joke with anyone interested in hearing one.

Clint also had incredible memorization skills. In High School, he was in a mainstream Biology Class. After the test for the Periodic Tables, Clint's teacher sent a note home letting me know that Clint, without help or modification, had scored a 99 on his test. It was the highest in the class. It just defied logic. Clint had an IQ of 60, with that IQ, his academic abilities should have paralleled, but they did not always. Many a time, they far exceeded expectation.

Another time, Clint had a spelling test coming up. I was testing him to see if he was ready. There were twenty words on the list. I started with the first one and went through them. Clint spelled them all perfectly.

I said, "I bet you learned those in order. We are going to go through them one more time backwards to make sure you know them."

So, I started at the twentieth word and planned to go backward to the first word on the list. When I gave Clint the twentieth word, without hesitation, he spelled the word backwards, perfectly. I was amazed. I did not say anything, I just continued up the list with the rest of the words. With each one, Clint spelled them backward, as well as he had spelled them forward. I said, "Clint, no more studying these. You are ready for your test for sure. "

When Clint turned sixteen, he received his driver's license. He took Driver's Education and memorized the book. Clint could not easily follow multi-stepped directions, so a map would be out of the question, but he passed the test. He was proud of that license. However, he never asked to drive. That was probably a good thing, honestly.

Through it all, Clint did well and was generally accepted by his peers. Unfortunately, adults were not always as kind. I remember one specific time when Clint was five and played Tee-ball. He got a hit but got mixed up running the bases and ran to third instead of first. One of the other parents in the stands looked at me and said, "I think it is just wonderful that they let kids like him play."

"What? What do you mean by kids like him?" That is what I wanted to say, along with, "I think it is equally as wonderful that they let people like you out in public." But didn't; I bit my tongue instead.

Occasionally, there were some kids who were mean, too, but honestly very few. Most people who met Clint and got to know him loved him. And he returned that love. He had the sweetest nature and never met anyone that he did not like. Generally speaking, the other kids would help him and were nice to him. However, he never really got invited to parties or extracurricular activities. As a result, his family—me, his grandparents, and aunts and uncles—were an important part of his inner circle.

Even with all of that, Clint was always good-natured and very thoughtful and mindful of doing what was right and what he was supposed to do. He was a people pleaser, never wanting anyone to be mad at him for anything. He was always helpful. In fact, he seldom complained about anything. He shook off whatever was bothering him very quickly. He had the most positive attitude and a genuine love for people, and found something good in everyone he met. You rarely would hear Clint bad-mouth anyone.

When Clint was little and he did something wrong, it was almost impossible to scold him. He always had real remorse. It would just break my heart. He would say things like, "Mom, I am so sorry I acted that way. Please forgive me."

I can tell you it is difficult to stay mad at someone, not to mention punish someone, who feels so bad when they do wrong.

CHAPTER 2

In 2000, when Clint was ten, I met Max in a computer chat room. That was before the advent of Facebook. I was living in Guntersville, Alabama. Max, a bachelor who had never married before, was living in Toronto, Ontario, Canada.

I had my computer for about a week and was fascinated by the Web. I had heard people talking about chat rooms and was curiously trying to see what that was about. At that time, chat rooms were popular, and all the "rooms" I tried to enter were full. I then saw a room entitled "Canadians-English." I was able to enter it and thought it would be cool to learn something about Canada. It was not a dating site, just a group of people talking to each other about Canadian things.

For those who are not familiar with the way chat rooms worked, when you initially went into a chat, you had to set up a profile which included your email or screen name and anything else you wanted to include. There was a place to put down your favorite quote. My quote was something like "Remember the giant oak was once just a nut that held its ground." Since I had gone through a rocky divorce a few years prior and started my life over, that quote just seemed to suit me.

I entered the chat room and was only observing all the back-and-forth conversations. Since I really knew nothing about Canada, I never even spoke. But when I went into the room, it showed that a "New screen name" had joined. Max looked at my profile and sent me an instant message, saying, "Cool quote." And that was how it began.

Back in those days, when you logged into your computer, others could see that you were online. So, after the initial contact, every time he or I would get the computer at the same time, we would casually chat back and forth. When I say "casually", it truly was. He would ask me about the weather in Alabama and tell me about the snow in Canada. We would talk about football and hockey, music, dogs, etc. It was just random, short, vague conversations. We did that for months. Then one Friday night, we happened to catch each other online and we talked for hours. He finally asked me if he could call me. We spent another two hours on the phone that night. I think he was amazed by my accent, his first encounter with a true southern girl, and, in honesty, I was a little smitten with his accent too. The conversation flowed easily; it was like talking to an old friend. From that night on Max and I spoke online or on the phone every night, lots of nights not getting off the phone until the wee hours of the morning and then both getting up for work the next day.

In November of that year, we were talking when Max told me that he was falling in love with me. I stopped dead in my tracks, silent, and then I realized that I loved him too. I said, "That's a problem, though. You are in Canada, and I am in Alabama, and we've never even met."

"That's no problem. I have a holiday coming up. I am going to come and visit you!"

When I told my friends and my parents that Max was coming, they freaked out. My mom said, "How do you know that he isn't an axe-murderer? You've met him on the computer and don't even know him."

But that was not true. I did know him. We had spent hours upon hours just talking without any outside distractions. It was just him and me, one on one, talking. I am usually very leery, but in this case, I was completely confident that something good was about to happen.

The week after Christmas, Max traveled the eighteen hours from Ontario to Alabama and stayed for a two-week visit. Max was very handsome, tall and muscular, with dark hair and a crooked smile that was endearing. He had never been to the South. We spent those two weeks celebrating the New Year, visiting Graceland, touring North Alabama, hanging out and getting to know each other better. I was right; he was the one. On his last night, he gave me a diamond "promise" ring and stole my heart.

I was very apprehensive when I started dating Max. Up until that point, it had been only Clint and me for the past three years. We were settled into our routine and I was a little worried about how well he and Max would accept each other. I told Max that Clint and I were a package deal and that he could not be in my life unless he was able to love Clint too.

Max replied, "I would not be able to love you if it were any other way. I already expected that you were a package deal."

Approaching their first meeting, Max was nervous, I could tell. He was worried that Clint would not like him. He brought Clint a Toronto Maple Leaf's hockey jersey and an expensive trick yo-yo. While he was here, he spent time throwing a ball with Clint and including him in everything that we did. Almost instantly they bonded.

In February, Clint stayed with my parents and I flew to Toronto and spent four days. In April Max flew back to Alabama for a week. In between we racked up hundreds of dollars in phone bills. Max returned to Alabama in May for what was supposed to be another visit, but that turned out to be permanent. Shortly after he arrived, I discovered that I was pregnant with a baby girl.

In June 2001, Max and I were married at my parent's house at the lake. Clint, dressed in a little suit and tie, walked me down the aisle and gave me away.

In September of that year, the biggest terrorist attack in history happened. I was seven months pregnant. I will never forget that day or how afraid I felt for my baby. In the weeks that followed, America rallied. Patriotism was everywhere; that was amazing to see. Max commented that he felt he had picked the worst time to immigrate to America, three months before the most infamous terrorist attack in history. I commented that I disagreed and believed he had picked the best time. He was living and seeing the best of America, in the aftermath of such tragedy. In November, Jessica Laine was born. Our family was complete.

The first year of our marriage was tough. There was love but our relationship had been a whirlwind and we got married quickly. It turned out to be quite a culture shock, especially for Max. He went from being a carefree bachelor in a huge city in another country to being a married father of two in a small town in Alabama. We were also navigating immigration and the challenges of having a newborn and Max was now around Clint every day as well. He was always good to Clint, but it was an adjustment, dealing with the day-to-day activities of a child with disabilities. They formed a fast friendship, and although it took a little longer to truly mesh it did happen. It was gradual and I am not sure exactly when it clicked, but Max and Clint eventually formed a true father-son relationship.

Max was a rough and tough man, but he had a big heart. He was stubborn to a fault. He played hockey and worked hard. He also worked with his hands. He could build or fix most anything. He was blunt and did not do fake; he would tell you just how it was, even when you did not necessarily want him to. But he always had such a way with Clint. He did not pity him. He treated him normally, setting boundaries and rules, he was disciplined with Clint and Clint respected him. Max also was very protective of Clint. That would prove to cause some intense moments between Max and Travis. Max also never missed any event or milestone of Clint's. Their love was palpable. Max was also an amazing father to Jessica. Being such a congenital tough guy, he melted around her. He called her his little princess, and she was.

Through all the changes, Clint was quite a trooper. His home life was spent between his dad's house and ours. I had custody of Clint, but his dad had visitation. That was always a struggle for us. Travis had a competitive nature. He did love Clint, but I also think he sometimes struggled with Clint's inability to do things that other boys his age did, like play sports, or other things that were age appropriate. He would often tell Clint he was disappointed in him for this or that. It really hurt Clint. He was also always trying to show us up with better gifts or better vacations, or by telling Clint that he did not have to listen to Max, because he was not his "dad." After every visitation, Clint would come home agitated and tired. We would have a struggle for a couple of days just to get him back into his routine.

His dad also spent a lot of time taking us to Court. It was always over custody and child support issues. He never got custody but would occasionally get his child support changed. In each of these endeavors, he would involve Clint. There were a lot of secrets, visits to lawyers, and court dates that became the norm for a few years. It would upset and confuse Clint, and he got to where he did not want to go to his dad's house for his visitations.

I was always worried about how these legal fees and court appointments would affect Max and our relationship. I worried because it was expensive and stressful, but I then realized that it affected him the same way it affected me on the day he told me that if we had to sell everything that we owned to pay the lawyer, that was what we would do. I saw the determination in his eyes.

Sometime in 2002, Max finally got his immigration work authorization and subsequently his green card. The next few years were filled with us doing what most people in their thirties do, in trying to build a home and career. Max got a job as a supervisor at the wastewater treatment plant in Huntsville. He also opened a side business building fences and decks. He worked long hours. I was still working for TVA. We bought a house in Arab, Alabama, a small, charming city about thirty miles south of Huntsville. Arab was located halfway between both of our jobs, which was a factor, but we also found out that the school system in Arab ranked amongst the best in the State, and that was a determining factor as well. The Special Education curriculum was especially great. I was excited about the opportunities this would afford Clint.

Jessica started to grow. She and Clint were eleven years apart in age. Initially, she idolized her big brother, looked up to him. Clint would read to her and try to teach her how to do things. She called him "Brutter." But by the time that Jessica turned nine or ten years old, it was evident that her cognitive abilities and academic abilities were exceeding those of what Clint was capable of. In elementary school, Jessica tested high enough intellectually to be placed in the gifted program. She was very smart. Suddenly, she could read and comprehend better than Clint. She could count money, ride a bicycle, and carry on a relevant conversation. It was at this point that she became acutely aware that Clint was different and of his disabilities.

Jessica always loved her brother and would be the first to defend him if someone else criticized or hurt him. But at the same time, they were siblings. So, she did not make a lot of time for him and honestly was not always kind. In fact, as she grew into a teenager, I believe she became a little jealous of the time I spent with Clint, and perhaps even became slightly ashamed of Clint. I think some of that was normal because, while the intellect was there, the maturity was not. But as a mother who loved them both, I was always torn between understanding her point of view and trying to protect Clint's feelings. It was a challenging balance.

Max and Clint's relationship continued to grow. Clint truly had a father figure with Max and Jessica had her dad wrapped around her finger. Max really loved being a family man and a father.

From the outside looking in, our lives would seem mundane. And it was for the most part. For years, we were all about work, school, yard work, grocery shopping and the like. Once a year we would slip away for a family vacation, but other than that, it was just the day-to-day grind. Clint continued to do well in school, as did Jessica. Other than the normal life stresses that affect everyone at one point or another, our life was pretty routine and uneventful.

CHAPTER 3

My parents, Woody and Noretta, lived within 30 miles of me my whole life. For over twenty-two years of that time, they had a lake house in Guntersville, right on the Tennessee River Main Channel. After Max and I were married, we spent just about every holiday and almost every weekend there. There was always dinner, music, boating or fishing, and usually a card game or two. It really became "the meeting" place. It was not uncommon for extended family or neighbors to be there as well. My mom and dad were warm and welcoming people by nature and their home was always open to anyone.

Clint and Jessica were their only grandchildren, and my parents took their role as grandparents to heart. They were always willing to babysit at the drop of a hat. My mom and Jessica would spend a lot of time doing crafts, making cookies, playing dress-up or walking down by the water finding shells.

My dad and Clint bonded from the time I brought Clint home from the hospital as a baby. My dad was so proud of Clint and had the most compassion and love for him. My dad was also the most patient person with Clint. He would take him fishing or to the barber's. He would also spend a lot of time out on the porch talking to Clint about whatever. Clint could tell his Pa-pooh about any struggles he was having. My dad also treated Clint like someone without disabilities. If Clint wanted to spend hours talking about Bruce Lee or his most recent video game, my dad, somehow, would stay engaged the entire time. He would ask questions and just listen. A lot of listening. You could tell that my dad thoroughly enjoyed the time. My dad was also very protective of Clint, and worried that the court battles between me and Travis was taking its toll on him. He spent a lot of time talking to Clint about that too and reassuring him that it would all be okay. Their relationship was special.

My dad always said, "If there were more people like Clint in this world, it would certainly be a better place."

My dad meant that, too, which pretty much summed up his relationship with Clint.

My dad had a repertoire of jokes, and most of them were bad, corny jokes, and, since my dad's name was Woody, we teasingly started calling his jokes "Wood Jokes." When he would tell them, we would all groan in unison and proclaim, "Ah, another Wood joke!!' The only one who did not do that was Clint. My dad would tell Clint his jokes and they would both laugh and laugh. Clint would try to learn jokes to tell my dad too. Many times, because of his disabilities, he would inevitably forget or mess up the punchlines. But it did not matter. They would laugh at those, too. Or they would try to figure out what the punchline should have been or end up making their own punchlines.

Through this, we realized that Clint really did have a sense of humor. His favorite joke was:

"What did the fish say when he swam into the wall? Dam!" And it did not matter how many times he told that joke (which was a lot), he and my dad would both laugh, as if it were the first time they had ever heard it.

The jokes were always one thing, but the best part of Clint's sense of humor was that many times he would just say something unintentionally funny. It would sneak up on you when you least expected. Clint often did not even realize he had said something funny, but he had delivered it with such timing you would think he was a comedian.

Once when Clint was young, he was in the living room playing quietly with a GI Joe figurine. The figurine was obviously made to look like a grown man.

Clint looked up and said, "Papooh, this is Joe. He's in the 9th grade."

My dad replied, "Clint, Joe looks awfully old to be in the 9th grade."

"Yeah, I know, He failed a bunch of grades."

Another hilarious conversation Clint had when he was a little older occurred when he decided that he did not like his middle name, Hollis. The name was my grandfather's and I always thought it was a great name, even though I suppose it is a little old-fashioned. But by this point, Clint had maintained for some time that he did not like it really. So, one day I asked him, "Clint, if you could change your middle name, what would you change it to?"

Clint had had years to think about this, so I was expecting him to say something like David, John, or Martin, or some other common name. Clint looked at me with a serious look on his face and said "Booger."

"Pardon?"

"Yes," Clint said, "I would change my name to Booger, Clinton Booger Williams."

"Really?"

He just grinned, and then broke into laughter. For several days after he would just go around the house saying, "My name is Clint, but you can just call me Booger."

CHAPTER 4

As Clint continued through school, our years were made up of a mixture of some mainstream classes, but mostly special education classes. During this time, The United States Congress, under the direction of President Bush passed the "No Child Left Behind" legislation. While probably well-intentioned, it really did not serve Clint well. There were certain rules that had to be followed regarding Special Needs Children, which took away the discretion of the teachers and parents to make decisions of each child individually. One such rule was that the top two percent of the special education students had to take standardized test with the rest of the student body, so that the school's end of the year numbers were not skewed. Clint always fell into this top two percentage, and once a year he would have to go through the timed, standardized testing with his mainstream friends. Clint was not allowed to have any help and had to struggle through. That was frustrating for us all. But overall, his Individual Education Plan (IEP) reports and teachers brought about a good balance with Clint's learning.

In 2009, Clint entered his senior year of high school. Such a great accomplishment. At the end of the school year, his school had a "Senior Award" night in which any child who had earned a scholarship or endowment was presented with it on that night. The students who earned these awards were to show up in their full caps and gowns, with guests to watch them get awarded. There was a lot of pomp, as there should have been. It was quite a big deal. Seniors who did not earn college recognition were not required to attend and typically did not. So, there was really no reason for Clint to be there.

On the week of the Awards Banquet, Clint's teacher called me and told me that Clint needed to wear a suit and his cap and gown and be present at the awards banquet. She also said that Max and I should plan to attend. She could not tell me why, but she wanted to make sure that we would all be there. We assured her that we would. We were perplexed, as we knew that Clint would not be awarded a scholarship. But when the time came, we dressed up and took our place in the audience. Clint sat handsomely with his peers in his suit and cap and gown.

When it came time to present the prestigious "Father Mike" award, the Arab Fire Department's Captain and Arab Fire Department Chief, dressed in their "dress" uniforms took the stage. They spoke of what the Father Mike award was. Father Mike was a New York City Fire Department Chaplain who was killed at the twin towers on 9-11 after he heroically went into the buildings to help people. An award was established in his honor to be given to an *Exceptional Special Education Student*, who exhibited courage and perseverance, and who was an all-around good person. Someone had nominated Clint for this award. The nomination for the recipient of this award was submitted by and voted on by the faculty (teachers and administrators) at the school. Clint walked up on stage in his cap and gown and accepted the award from the Fire Captain in front of his peers, family, and the teachers that had voted for him. What an incredibly proud day for all of us!

In 2009, the requirement for graduation was that every student, to receive a diploma, had to have a certain number of curriculum/class credits and also be able to pass a graduation exam without help or modification. There was no way for Clint to do this. But at the same time, Clint was excited and dedicated to completing his senior year and graduating. Technically, because of the requirements, he did not receive a diploma, but he did earn a Certificate of Completion. We never told him the difference. As he walked up on the stage in his cap and gown to receive his certificate, he was proud just the same, and he had honestly earned that moment.

That summer, without having school any longer, Max and I realized that Clint needed something else to do. When we talked to him about it, Clint said he would like to work just like we did. I started calling different businesses to see if that was an option. I finally contacted our local grocery store, Warehouse Discount Grocery (WDG) and spoke to the manager, Cindy.

"I was wondering if you hire persons with disabilities?"

To my surprise, Cindy said, "Can your son come in this afternoon for an interview?"

I was at work, so Max helped Clint pick out appropriate clothing and off they went for Clint's first ever interview. Max went inside with him. Cindy spent about 15 minutes talking to them both and then looked at Clint and said, "Can you start Friday?"

Clint started as a bag boy. He worked for a couple of hours, a couple of days a week. He loved it. He was proud of himself. And if he had to be at work at noon, he was up, showered and in uniform, ready to go by no later than nine am. Without fail.

But at first, Clint really did not know what he was supposed to do. I was not sure if he was going to be able to keep the job. Every day after work, when I picked him up, he would tell me how he accidently dropped something or how a customer had yelled at him for not bagging their groceries properly. I would inquire what Ms. Cindy had said to him, or if he had gotten into trouble. He would tell me "no." He told me that Ms. Cindy had encouraged him and tried to teach him. He also told me that he would see Ms. Cindy talking to the customer. I surmised that she was apologizing to them. As I later found out, she was not apologizing, she was explaining that Clint was still learning and had difficulties because of his disabilities, yet he was here trying. She would tell the customer that being mean or disrespectful towards Clint was unacceptable... Cindy stood by Clint, taught him, took up for him, encouraged him, and never gave up on him. There are genuinely good people in the world, Cindy being one of them. From that point on, she and the grocery store had our unwavering loyalty.

Clint had been working there for a couple of months when one day I picked him up and he announced proudly, "Mom, I learned something today, something very important!"

"You did? What?"

Clint looked at me very seriously and said, "I learned bread ALWAYS goes on the top!"

I had to bite my tongue not to laugh. It was another of those times where Clint was not meaning to be funny. But since then, that simple thought keeps things in perspective for me during the times when I am struggling to understand something that may seem obvious to others, I mumble to myself, "Bread always goes on the top," just as a reminder that I can get it, just as Clint had.

Later that year, my parents decided to sell their house on the lake and move to Arab to be closer to us. I was surprised by the move, but my dad was having a hard time keeping up with the chores and lawn at the lake house. My mom said that he had been diagnosed with some heart issues and was slowing down a bit. The whole thing was kind of vague and while I did not really understand entirely, I was thrilled that they were living closer.

Coincidently, the house they bought was literally two streets over from Clint's work. This proved to be helpful. If Clint ever had to be at work during mine or Max's work hours, my mom or dad would just take him or pick him up and he would go to their house until we got home. This went on for a couple of years. Clint and mom and dad became even closer if that was possible. As a result of Clint's perseverance and mom's and dad's help, Clint worked for two years straight without taking a day off or being late. He continued to learn and made less mistakes. The few times he would make a mistake or upset a customer, Cindy continued to take up for him. I was grateful that he had a caring place to be, had a purpose. He continued to be ready for work hours before he had to be there. If there was ever inclement weather and he had to skip work, it would upset him. He would get mad if you even suggested that he miss a day of work for vacation or for anything.

In early summer of 2011, my dad came to me and said that something had been on his mind. He told me that he thought I should have Clint's disabilities re-tested. He pointed out that with Clint being able to work, and with his sense of humor, and his memorization skills, he thought that there may be a misdiagnosis.

I listened to him intently and then replied, "Dad, I don't know how to get him retested or where to take him for that. What are you thinking it is?"

He said, "I don't know, but what if it isn't cognitive disabilities? What if it is something else, like a form of autism or some medical condition?"

"That could be possible, I suppose, but the outcome is the same. So regardless of the label, what difference would it make it this point?"

Dad continued, "I don't know, but what if there is something we can do to help him and we just don't know what it is? What if there is medicine or something that would help him learn better?" he paused. "I know it is probably a long shot, but I know that Clint has so much more going on than what they've said."

"I hear you, Dad, but again, I wouldn't even know where to begin and I am not sure that there is a magic pill...."

He then asked me if he could just do some research and I told him that he could. A couple of weeks later, he came over for coffee, he had printed all kind of things out about autism and cognitive disabilities and different resources. I was grateful but did not give it a lot of attention at that time. I thanked him and set everything aside, with the full intention of going through it all later.

CHAPTER 5

In March 2011, Clint was about to turn twenty-one. And I must say, I learned a valuable lesson while planning for his birthday, which was to never underestimate how kind people can truly be. I will preface by saying that I had seen a lot of kindness extended throughout the years, but kids (and perhaps their parents) are not always very accepting of people who are different. So, after Clint started school, even though there were many who were kind to him, he was usually excluded from other kids' birthday parties. He never had a lot of kids interested in coming to his either. It saddened me, but there was not much I could do about it. So, whenever Clint's birthday rolled around, we (the family) always celebrated and made it as special as we could for him, even though I am sure that it was not the same for him as having a "real" party.

But this year, Clint's twenty-first, was a much-anticipated birthday for him, a big deal. Max and I wanted it to be extra special. Clint was always talking about "his friends" at work, so we decided that we would take Clint out to dinner and see if any of his co-workers may be interested in joining us. I called Cindy to discuss our plans, and she said she would ask around and let me know. We decided to keep it a secret from Clint, just in case no one came, so that he would not be disappointed.

A couple of days later, I called Cindy back to follow-up. She said that she had asked around but did not remember the number of people; however, a few had said they would try to come. That was a little vague. Max and I reserved a space at the local BBQ place. We were expecting about eight family members and then just hoped that two or three others from Clint's work may come. We really did not know what to expect, but had our fingers crossed that it would be a nice surprise for him.

Clint spent the day at my parents' house. We told him that we would try to meet up with them and go out to eat for his birthday. Other than that, no one did anything special for him during the day (which was harder on his "Nanny" than on him, I assure you). So, he thought that going out to dinner with us was all that was going to happen for his twenty-first birthday.

Max and I arrived at the restaurant a little early to bring Clint's cake. When we arrived, the hostess led us to a back private room of the restaurant. When she opened the door, to our surprise, the entire room was full of people. They were all there for Clint. In addition to family, some of our neighbors came, and fourteen people from Clint's work (plus there were two others who could not come that sent gifts). In all, there were about twenty-five people at his party. He was so surprised!

It was beautiful to see the way he and his co-workers interacted. They were all laughing and kidding around with Clint. They all came to celebrate with him—they did not have to—they wanted to. Clint was accepted, included, and, in fact, he was the star of the party. It was awesome to be a part of, and, if you were to ask Clint, I believe he would tell you that this was his best birthday ever!

CHAPTER 6

In July of 2011, Max and I planned our vacation, working around Clint's work schedule, of course. And as we had done for three years, we included my mom and dad in our plans. In the past years we had been to Sanibel Island and Disney World in Florida, to Tunica Mississippi and to Charleston/Myrtle Beach, South Carolina. My mom and dad liked to go to places but shortly before they moved to Arab, my dad proclaimed that he did not think he could make long drives on his own any longer. Again, no explanation was ever given to me or Max, but we just assumed that considering my parents' age this was normal. We enjoyed including them and having them with us anyway, especially Clint and Jessica.

For our annual vacation, we planned to go to Biloxi, Mississippi and to Gulf Shores, Alabama. We were all looking forward to the trip, especially my dad. He was looking forward to taking Clint to a casino for the first time. I am not sure that Clint understood the concept, but my dad looked forward to sharing the time with Clint and he also thought going to the casino was a rite of passage for Clint since he had turned twenty-one. My dad had also been looking forward to us all eating seafood and being on the coast.

We rented a van and headed out on Sunday, July 17. We arrived in Biloxi around supper time. We all went out to eat together and then took turns between going to the casino and staying in the room with Jessica, (playing games, watching TV, etc.). Monday when we went for breakfast, Jessica complained that her ear hurt. We called our doctor at home in Arab and asked him to call in a prescription to a pharmacy in Biloxi.

After we finished eating, Max, Jessica, and I went into town. We took Jessica to see a movie and then went and picked up her medicine, we also did some shopping. We did not get back to the room until around supper. While we were gone, Mom, Dad and Clint went to the casino. My dad had given Clint twenty dollars and he won a hundred and thirty-five. Clint was excited and so was my dad.

On Tuesday, we left Biloxi and headed the ninety miles to Gulf Shores. At night we all went out to eat fresh gulf seafood. My dad had been talking about eating seafood for weeks. After we ate, we got back to the cottage. I got our laundry (from Biloxi) out of the van so I could wash clothes while mom, dad, Max, and I played a couple of card games of Rook.

On Wednesday we went out to get into the van and we spotted a pair of men's underwear in the parking lot. We all commented and joked about how disgusting it was that someone would leave their underwear in the parking lot. We could only imagine what they were doing that would have prompted the underwear to wind up there in the first place.

We all piled into the van and headed out for our day's adventure to Ft. Morgan, a military war fort, we then rode the ferry over to Dauphin Island. This was my dad's idea, he grew up in Mobile and when he and my mom were dating, they used to go to Ft. Morgan and picnic and over to Dauphin Island to the beach, He thought the kids would really enjoy seeing it. During the day, dad reminisced about proposing to my mom and about all the fishing trips he, my granddad, and my brother, Jim, used to go on. He pointed out all "the spots" he remembered and discussed how much it all had changed. We enjoyed the excursion, but it was extremely hot, and going to see all of that took most of the day. So, we were all exhausted. Once we were back on the ferry, Jessica started complaining that her ear was hurting again; the medicine we had gotten her was not working. We could tell that she obviously did not feel well, and she started running a temperature.

We got back to the cottage and as we were getting out of the van, my mom and dad and Jessica went ahead towards the cottage, while Max and I retrieved our belongings from the van. As we did this, we noticed that the underwear was still lying in the parking lot, and upon a little closer examination, I realized that they were Clint's underwear. Apparently, they had fallen out of the laundry bag the night before.

My Dad went ahead of us and was sitting on the stairs of the cottage, waiting for us to come around from the car with the key, when we turned the corner with underwear in hand and told him that "They were Clint's." Dad burst into laughter. He and Clint joked the rest of the night about "Clint's drawers being out in the parking lot for everyone to see."

Once we got settled into our cottage, Max and I started trying to find a hospital to take Jessica to have her ear checked. We found out that there were no hospitals in Gulf Shores; the closest one was thirty miles away in the town of Foley. Dad and I discussed how bad that could be if someone had a real emergency. After a lengthy search, we eventually found a walk in Clinic that was still open, to take Jessica. The doctor examined her and determined she had a bad ear infection. He prescribed a stronger medicine for her. We left and got back to the cottage around 9:00 pm.

On Thursday morning, Jessica woke me up around 7:00 am. She was crying because her ear was hurting. Mom and Dad were already up outside sitting on the porch. I could tell they had not been up long because the coffee was still brewing. I gave Jessica her medicine and some Tylenol and she fell back asleep on the couch.

Dad seemed very anxious and out of sorts. He was a little grumpy and told me that he had not slept well and was going to go back for a nap after breakfast, but he and I were also talking about other things too, like Jessica not feeling well and whether she would be up for the beach, which was our tentative plan for the day.

Mom went for a shower and my dad got up and started washing dishes. This was so out of character for him. He normally was not a "dish doer." While it seemed odd to me, I did not give much thought to it at the time. My dad was making a lot of noise with the clanking of dishes, which woke Max up. Max thought it was me who was making so much noise. So, when he came out of the bedroom, he shot me a look and made a sarcastic remark to the effect that eight in the morning would sure be a good time to be sleeping if you were, say, on vacation.

And while this comment was unnecessary for sure, Max really did not mean much by it.

Max and I had been married for over ten years at this point. An occasional banter with him wasn't uncommon. However, he would have never said that had he realized that it was my dad who had been washing dishes. Max said his piece to me and grabbed a cup of coffee and headed back to our room to jump in the shower and start the day.

Dad stormed out to the porch. He was obviously mad. I followed. He said, "Who licked the red off of Max's candy this morning?"

"Dad, he didn't know you were the one making the noise. He is not mad; he is just still half-asleep. After he drinks his coffee and gets dressed; he will be in a better mood. Don't worry about it."

He then stated, "No, he has been an asshole all week."

This statement caught me off guard. It was completely out of character for my dad but was also simply not true. I was taken aback by it.

I said, "Dad, that's not true. Max thought it was me this morning, but he hasn't been an ass at all. He has given you car to door service at every destination; he has carried your luggage, gone on the day trips you wanted to go on, etc. Max has been good to you all week. He just started out this morning on the wrong side of the bed. Please, just let it go."

"No, that isn't true. Last night, I was sitting in the room and you and he went to bed and turned the lights out on me. You didn't even say good night, just left me alone, sitting in the dark."

"Dad, what the hell are you talking about? You and mom went to bed almost two hours before we did last night. We never left you sitting alone in the dark."

"Oh, yes you did!!" he continued, "and, I have had enough of all this. If I had my own car with me, I'd just go home right now!"

I will admit at this point I was not thinking about why he was behaving this way; I was just getting pissed off.

"What? Dad, don't let not having a car stop you. If that is the way you feel, go and pack your stuff, and I will drive you home myself!" I stormed into our bedroom where Max had just gotten out of the shower and was getting dressed.

When I walked in, he smiled and said, "Morning."

He was not even thinking about the earlier interaction. As far as he was concerned, it was over. Nor did he know what had just happened between me and my dad. I recounted the conversation to him and asked why my dad was so angry with him.

He said, "I don't know. I have no idea, but we are on vacation; we will work it out."

He finished dressing and headed out to the porch to speak to my dad. Max walked out and my dad was still sitting on the porch, stewing. Max said, "Sorry if I was short this morning. I thought it was Paula washing dishes. I didn't realize it was you because I was just waking up. Again, sorry I didn't mean anything by it."

Dad barked, "It wasn't just this morning. You left me in the dark last night. In fact, you have been an asshole for this whole trip!"

I was still upset but now Max was also getting defensive. He raised his voice a little when he said, "What? What are you even talking about?"

Then my mom and Clint walked out. My mom could tell there was a lot of tension. She asked what was going on. My dad said to her, "Go inside and see if you can find us a rental car. I want to go home."

She said, "Why?"

"Don't ask questions. Just go inside and look for a place to rent a car right now!" My mom was clearly confused too but turned and went back inside.

Max spoke again asking my dad why he was acting so irrationally. My dad started arguing his points again. Then suddenly, he just stopped and said, "Let's just continue this later. I am not feeling well."

He instantly turned very pale and leaned over in the chair and put his head in his hands. Going from angry to concerned, I said, "Dad, just stay here, I am going to go get you a cold towel, it is hot out here."

I went in and got a towel and told my mom that Dad was not feeling well. As I turned around my dad and Max were coming inside. My dad sat down on the couch and I gave him the cold towel. At this point he was still pale, sweating, and clearly struggling with his breathing, almost hyperventilating. I told him to calm down. Without hesitation, my mom called 9-11. Max went out to meet the ambulance.

In just moments, my dad was not able to speak. I said to him, "Oh my God, Dad. I am so sorry I got mad at you." With tears running down my face, I continued, "Dad, please be okay. I love you."

Dad looked at me with a fear in his eyes that I will never forget. He could not speak but he clearly mouthed, "I love you too." He then slumped over and lost consciousness. Max was still outside waiting for the ambulance. My mom started screaming, "Help him!"

Clint and Jessica were both just staring in frightened disbelief. Somehow, I got my dad off the couch and onto the floor and immediately started CPR. In a few minutes the volunteer fire department from Ft. Morgan arrived. They continued with CPR until finally the paramedics arrived from Foley, which was about thirty miles away.

My mom rode with dad in the ambulance. Max, the kids, and I got everything locked up and followed in our car. We arrived at the hospital probably twenty minutes after the ambulance.

When we arrived at the hospital, the security guard stopped me from going to where my dad was, saying that a nurse would be coming to get me in a moment. I had a bad feeling. Then the nurse appeared, and I knew. She took me back to my mom.

My dad did not make it. He died in the ambulance, en route to the hospital. I do not remember much except just screaming and crying. They led us all into a chapel to wait for the doctor and coroner to come and talk to us. We spent hours in that chapel. It took a long time to for them to make arrangements and finalize things.

Mom and I talked about the morning and what had happened. My dad had told her earlier, before I even woke up, that he was not feeling well. He had also told her that Max and I had left him in the dark the night before and that he was mad at us. She did not know what he was talking about either, but assumed that maybe he had gotten back up after she fell asleep. I told her that he had not. He was still in bed when we went to bed.

Neither she nor I caught the signs, but in hindsight, we believe he was already having trouble. We just did not realize it. The coroner ruled the cause of death Flash Pulmonary Edema. He had an episode, not sure if it was a heart attack or what, but his lungs started filling with fluid quickly. After he passed, my mom confessed that my dad had been diagnosed for a couple of years with Congestive Heart Failure. She said that he realized he was on borrowed time. He did not want any of us to know how sick he was and worry. He just wanted to spend time with us and not be fussed.

After he died, we all went back to the cottage. My dad's clothes were scattered all over his room. The cards we played and snacks we had enjoyed the night before were still sitting in the kitchen area. The living room was disheveled where the paramedics had done their work. We were just in shock, in grief, lost. We were discussing an exit plan to get back home when Jessica appeared with my dad's suitcase. Max asked her what she was doing, and she responded that she had packed up her Pa-pooh's stuff so we could go home to be with our family. She was only nine. The six-hour drive home, in a van, missing one, was the longest six hours of my life. I do not think any of us spoke a word all the way home.

My dad was laid to rest on Monday July 25. His Eulogy was given by his best friend of over 55 years, Brother Donald Davis. At the graveside, The United States Air Force Honor Guard folded and presented the American Flag to my mom as a lone bugler played "Taps." All my dad's family and friends were there, either in person or in spirit. My dad was honored, and he would have been so proud.

I was a grown woman, albeit a daddy's girl. I had always spent every Christmas, every Thanksgiving (and Canadian Thanksgiving), gone on vacations, and generally just hung out with my dad a lot. He was always my biggest supporter, cheerleader, and advocate. My dad believed in God and his faith was strong. My children could not have had a better grandfather. Pa-pooh was the best. He loved Clint and Jessica both so much. He was also a loving husband, as he and my mom had been married for fifty-two years. I am grateful for the time I had with my dad and all the memories. I look at them as blessings, but I would be lying if I said that my heart was not broken.

The night after my dad passed away, back at home, I found myself alone in my bedroom, sobbing uncontrollably and saying somewhat to myself—or to God, or to my dad, I am really not sure— "Dad, I feel so bad about your death. I just wish I knew or had a sign that everything would be okay."

Right at that moment, Clint appeared virtually from nowhere, saying, "Mom, are you upset about Pa-pooh?"

"Yes."

Clint then looked at me and spoke for just a moment as someone without any disability, almost as if someone else was speaking, "Pa-pooh has a healthy body now. It was his time to be in heaven. Mom, his name was in the book of life," he continued, "Don't cry. I am going to sit beside you on the bed until you fall asleep, but mom, it's going to be okay."

The next day I went to my mom's house to be with incoming family and friends. When I came back home that evening, there was a very bright yellow feather lying by the back door. I made note of it because it seemed so out of place there on the carport. By the next day, the feather had slipped my mind. I was in auto pilot, doing what needed to be done, preparing for my dad's funeral, the service, visiting with family.

The following week when I went back to work, I was talking to a coworker about my dad's passing and the funeral. In the conversation, I mentioned to him what had happened with Clint the night after dad died. I told him that I was not sure if that was a sign, but I felt like my dad was sending me a message, and because my dad and Clint were so close, I felt that Clint had been used as an instrument for that.

He said that he thought that was possible and then recounted a story that happened to his wife after her mother had died. He told me that after her funeral, his wife was in her bedroom grieving when out of nowhere a feather floated down from the ceiling. He said to that day they still did not know where the feather came from, but they felt that it was a sign from her mother and so she kept that feather. As soon as he told me that story, my mind went back to the week prior and the bright yellow feather at my back door. *Hmm*, I wondered, *could that have been a sign too?*

After that conversation, I started seeing feathers constantly. In the weeks following, every time I felt sad or overwhelmed, a feather appeared. I saw them in the parking lot at work, in my backyard, at the grocery store, while away on a business trip. Different kinds of feathers. One day I was outside at work and looked down and there was a chicken feather. Once I saw that feather, I just burst out laughing. Now, I still do not know if that was a sign from my dad or not, but with his sense of humor, it would certainly make sense. Either way, a sign or a just coincidence, I must admit, I found comfort in the sight of a feather.

CHAPTER 7

The days after my dad died seem to blur in my memory. My mom tried to get everything organized and figure out what the new normal was. We did much the same. We were all just going through the motions.

I sunk into a great depression. I was overcome with guilt. I was angry that I did not know about my dad's illness ahead of time. I felt shame that we had a fight the morning of his death. I was mad at myself for not realizing that something was wrong; the argument was so out of character for my dad, and I did not recognize it, thus I did not seek help sooner. Also, I felt that perhaps had we not argued, he would not have had a heart episode. Maybe it was stress that caused it. I then got it into my head, in a warped sort of way, that by me stressing him out, I had killed him. And lastly, I doubted whether I had performed CPR correctly, was there something I could have done differently? The weeks following my dad's death were a living hell for me. I was not kind to myself. My brain would not stop replaying the day of my dad's death over and over. Max and my mom became very worried about my state of mind and wellbeing. My mom suggested that I go and talk to my doctor.

It took me months to finally take her advice. I think I wanted to feel rotten. I deserved it. Self-consciously, I think I was glad to be living in my guilt and depression to punish myself for letting my dad down. For the first time in my life, I was even possibly suicidal. Clint and Jessica were the only thing that squashed those thoughts from my mind. I had never experienced a deep depression like that in my life. I realized my mom was right—I needed help.

I made an appointment with my doctor. When he came into the room, I calmly ask him if he knew anything about Flash Pulmonary Edema and Congestive Heart Failure. When he responded that he did know some, I just broke down in an uncontrollable sob and blurted out, "My dad had that—we argued, I stressed him out, and I killed him. It was my fault that he died!"

"Whoa, wait a minute," the doctor said.

He put my chart down and pulled his chair up so that he and I were sitting face to face about two foot apart. He looked me directly in the eye and said, "Okay, calm down, and let's start over, please tell me what you are talking about?"

I recounted the events of the whole day that my dad died to him. He listened very patiently to everything I had to say. He then explained that even though the episode seemed to have happened quickly, the fluid had been probably building up in my dad's lungs for at least twenty-four hours prior, which is why he had told my mom he was not feeling well. He went on to explain that as a result, he probably was not getting enough oxygen to the brain already and that is why he was confused and being irrational and saying things that had not actually happened. He also reassured me by telling me that he felt had my dad lived, he probably would not have even remembered that morning or the argument at all, and if he did, he would have felt bad about what he had said. He further assured me that I had in fact not killed my dad.

We also discussed the CPR. I was certified in CPR through my job at TVA. As a matter of fact, I had to take recertification every two years, so I had taken CPR training five or six times. I went through all that I had done. I told the doctor that I doubted myself, felt like there was something I had missed, something else I should have done. We went over everything step by step and he assured me that I had done everything exactly right.

Lastly, he recommended that I allow him to put me on an anti-depressant for a short period to get through the time of grief. He hugged me and told me to be kinder to myself. He said, "I can tell how much you loved your dad, and I can assure you that he knew it and loved you too."

That visit, his advice and the medication did help me. The lesson was learned as well. I would never again be so easily provoked to anger and misunderstanding with anyone. I also took comfort that my last words to my dad and his to me ultimately were that we loved each other.

CHAPTER 8

In September, my mom told me that the adjustment of losing my dad was hard. She had married and moved in with my dad, straight from her parents' home. I had not realized or ever really thought about it before, but in her seventy years, it was the first time she had ever lived alone. Max and I and the kids rallied around. The kids would spend the night with her more often and Max and I bought my mom a little dog to keep her company, a shih tzu that she named Mishy.

In November, just four months after my dad passed, tragedy happened again. We received a phone call that my Uncle Ed, my mom's only sibling, had a major heart attack. He was sitting at the computer at his house in Tennessee when he just slumped over in his seat. My cousins who were with him did CPR and got him to the hospital, but the brain damage was extensive, and he died two weeks later.

My Uncle Ed was career Navy, having served over thirty years, and upon his passing, we were informed that he would have the honor of being buried in Arlington National Cemetery in Washington DC. Even though he died in November, the ceremony did not take place until January. My mom could not drive to Washington from Alabama, especially not in the winter, and not by herself. Max and I told her that we would take her.

When the time came, we both took the week off from work. The funeral was on Thursday. We spent the whole day at Arlington. It was such a serene place and my uncle's funeral was flawless. It was handled with such precision. It seems wrong to say I enjoyed a funeral, but, honestly, his service was one of the coolest things I have ever seen; it was very reverent.

The rest of the week, we had decided to take mom, Clint, and Jessica to see some of the landmarks in Washington. We had set up appointments to meet with our congressman, tour the pentagon, the capital, and some of the war monuments. In Washington, as in all big cities, there are cabs, and public transportation, and we took advantage of a lot of that. But there are also so many landmarks within walking distance of each other, so we did a lot of walking too.

We noticed that my mother really struggled with the walking. She had to sit a lot and rest and catch her breath. My mom was a little overweight and out of shape. We realized that, as a result of her weight, the walking was wearing her out. We remained patient with her, but she would tire quickly. At some point during the trip, we even borrowed a wheelchair so we could push her around for the bigger excursions.

A month later, in February, my first cousin, George, on my dad's side, had a stroke and subsequently passed away. He was young, in his fifties. He was a professor at a College in Virginia and his funeral was conducted there. My mom wanted to go to his service as well. But since Max and I had taken a week of vacation to Gulf Shores, another week off when dad passed and a week to go to Washington in just the past five months, there was no way that we could take off any more time to take her. My dad's brother, Quitman, his wife Lou, and my cousin and her family were going. They said my mom could ride with them. Mom told me when she got back that she just did not realize how much walking there would be at the college. She said that the school provided a golf cart and chauffeured her and my aunt Lou around the campus. She said, "I guess I am just getting old, but I just couldn't do all of the walking."

In March, my mom started having trouble with gas and shortness of breath. She went to the doctor and was diagnosed with acid reflux and given medicine for indigestion. At that time, she told me that she was going to give that a chance to work, but she did not think it was indigestion or reflux, she had a feeling that something else was wrong.

CHAPTER 9

For the next few months, we all just went through the motions. Max and I were working every day, coming home, and spending time with Jessica at the softball field. Every other bit of time we had, we tried to spend with mom. She would come to our house, or we would all meet and go out to eat. One afternoon we went to Desoto State park for a picnic. It was a nice day.

Mom also tried to keep herself busy. She joined in a couple of civic clubs and a quilting club. She was making some friends and finding things to occupy her days. She also eventually embraced having her new little dog. When we first got her Mishy, she would get annoyed. It was tough on mom having a puppy, and having to get used to feedings and getting up in the middle of the night for potty trips, and having to house train, etc. Mom said it was like having a baby in the house again. Many days she would call me exasperated and say, "I think I just need to find her another home."

But then by the next day she would call to tell me what cute thing Mishy had done. I could tell the two of them were starting to bond. Having Mishy was good for my mom, as much as she complained, that little dog entertained her and gave her a purpose. And every time mom went out, she would come in with something new for that dog, a sweater, dog toys, or an occasional McDonald's hamburger. Honestly, I have seen children who do not get treated as well as that little dog did.

Clint was still working at the grocery store, by this point, he had been there for a couple of years. He still got up and got ready hours before having to be there. He was still as enthusiastic about it as he was when he first got the job. I was just thrilled that he had the job, kind of the same way Mishy gave mom a purpose, working at the grocery store gave Clint a purpose. He would amaze me, too. It was not uncommon for me to pick him up after work and he would be carrying a grocery bag of stuff. I would ask what he had, and he would respond with some random thing, such as, "It's trash bags," or "dishwashing detergent," or "coffee for you, mom. I noticed this morning you were getting low at home, so I bought some."

At the same time, to pay for those things, he would just hand the cashier money and let them give him change back. He never really knew what they gave him or if the change was right. He could not count it, nor did he understand the value of it. That always concerned me, that someone would take advantage of him. But to my knowledge, no one ever did. His coworkers accepted Clint and always helped him.

Clint would also still have an occasional customer who would complain about him for being slow, or not bagging their groceries the way they liked, or dropping something. Each time that happened, I would worry that he was not doing well at the store, but he would assure me that Ms. Cindy took up for him and then would help him figure out what he had done wrong, so he could do better. I was just grateful to her for giving Clint the job and opportunity and for being so sweet to him always.

One day while I was at work, my phone rang, and I saw on caller ID that it was Cindy. I was kind of nervous of why she was calling, I worried that Clint had done something wrong. When I answered, she said, "I just wanted to let you know that earlier today Clint was talking to some of the cashiers and was complaining to them that he had been here for years and never gotten a promotion."

"Oh, Cindy, I am so sorry. I will talk to him. We are grateful for the job that he has."

She interrupted me, "No, he is right. He has been working for me for years, is always on time, tries hard, and does good job every time he is here. We love him. And I believe he earned a promotion, so I just wanted call and let you know that I promoted him from bagger to fronter today." She continued, "He will now be responsible for making sure that all the groceries are at the front of the shelves."

When I picked Clint up from work, he was elated. So was I. A few months later at the store's employee appreciation luncheon, Clint was presented with an award for "The Store's Best Fronter." When he got home, we framed it and hung it his room, where it stayed for years.

CHAPTER 10

My mom was an interesting person. She had a beautiful soul and a smile that would light up the room. She was raised in the 1940-50's by parents who were poor. She learned at an early age to cook and clean. She also learned to grow and harvest and can her own food. Due to the era in which she was raised, she also believed it was the women's roll to be the sole homemaker and the caretaker of the children. Growing up, it was always my mom who did all the cooking, laundry, and grocery shopping. I would say that she and my dad had the stereotypical roles of a couple married in 1960. But my mom was also independent, very smart, and would be the first to stand up for herself when she needed to. She also always worked outside of the home too. In fact, she was one of the hardest working people I knew. And she always did so without complaint.

My mom was also a fierce defender and advocate of her family. She loved us all deeply. She wore blinders when it came to us; mostly, she saw no fault. This was especially true where Clint and Jessica were concerned. They were perfect in her eyes and could do no wrong. There were no women ever born that took to the role of being a grandmother as well my mom did. I do not believe there was anything she would not do for either of them.

I was young when Clint was born, my mom would gladly help, babysit, advise, or just love. With Jessica, she was even more hands on. She would make clothes for Jessica and she made every Halloween costume Clint and Jessica ever had. She absolutely adored them both and the feeling was mutual. Because we lived so close, she literally saw them and spoke to them every week. She was at every single school function, play, or event. She went to see Jessica ride horses and play softball. On holidays and weekends, she expected us all to be at her house. She always cooked a big meal.

My mom was also one of those people who never got sick either. It was not uncommon for my dad to get the flu at least once a year or for me and my brother to have different ailments throughout. But I remember only very few times in my life that my mom even had a cold. She was just never sick, but she was always just taking care of us in some way or another.

After dad died, I started to see some cracks in her armor. For the first time ever, I saw a vulnerability I had never seen before. My mom started confiding in me fears she had about navigating life alone. She also started asking my opinion and advice on things. We would host her at our house for dinner and the kids would spend the night at her house on most weekends. We tried to keep her company.

In March 2012, I was at work when one of my mom's neighbors, Gay, called me to let me know that my mom was at the Emergency Room. Gay told me that she was walking around the block when she found my mom stranded at her mailbox. Mom was so short of breath that she could not walk back up the driveway to go inside. I left right away and joined my mom at the hospital.

The doctors at first thought maybe she was having some heart trouble or maybe pneumonia because of her shortness of breath. They ordered X-rays of her chest. When the results came back, the doctor came into the room and told my mom that the X-rays showed that her chest and heart were both clear, but there was a lot of fluid in her abdomen, the fluid was pushing against her lungs, which what was causing her difficulty in breathing.

I said, "Okay, what is causing that? And what does it mean?"

The doctor said, "It can be only one of two things; it is either cancer or cirrhosis of the liver."

"Cirrhosis of the liver? My mom doesn't drink…wait, did you say cancer?"

He continued, "She could have Cirrhosis, even without being a drinker. That is why we need to send her for further testing. If I were you, I would pray for it to be cancer in this case. If it is cirrhosis, there is nothing that can be done. But, if it is cancer, she may have a chance with treatment."

With that, they drained fluid off her belly, and sent us home to await many other doctor appointments and tests. They sent my mom to a Doctor who specializes in liver disorders and she also had an appointment with an Oncology OB GYN.

It was a long month awaiting the results, but in mid-April, they were in. My mom was diagnosed with Stage IV Ovarian Cancer. It was actually cancer of her peritoneal lining, which is the lining that surrounds all of the organs in the stomach. The tissue is akin to the tissue in the ovaries, and so, for medical purposes, it is considered the same. The news was not good, in fact, the diagnosis was grim. The oncologist gave us a little hope that with Chemotherapy and surgery perhaps she would go into remission, but he was clear that there would be no cure.

From that point on, my mom refused to look up anything or do any research regarding her illness. She did not read the statistics or other people's cancer testimonies; she did not think of the worst case. It was almost as if she did not know the information, it just did not exist. Instead, she committed to do whatever the doctor would have her do. She did not seem to hear or understand the word remission. Her spoken word to us was always "cured," even though that is not what the doctor said. Yet, no one corrected her. You know, hope is the one thing that you never want to take away from someone, especially when that is really all they have. She kept telling me not to worry.

She told me, "I am going to beat this and be around for Clint and Jessica, in fact," she continued, "I plan to see Jessica get married one day."

She almost had me believing that she would.

My mom began Chemo the week after diagnosis. At that time, a true and profound journey began between me and my mom. She was scared. We have all heard such terrible things about the horrors of chemo. And by the way, they are all true. I could not imagine what she must be feeling, only how I would feel if I were in her shoes. I promised her that I would be with her every step of the way.

Chemo was brutal. Over the next few weeks, my mom lost her color, her hair, her appetite, and a lot of weight. However, what she did not lose was her smile, her joy of life, her optimism, or her will to live. She handled her illness with such grace. I witnessed everything she was going through, and I knew the amount she was suffering. Yet, my mom still never complained.

In August 2012, my mom was admitted into Huntsville Hospital for a grueling surgery to remove the tumor from her abdominal cavity. The doctor removed a tumor he said was the size of a "trout." The surgery was major. She was in the hospital for several days and then came to stay with me and Max for the next seven weeks. I took a leave of absence from TVA and took care of her. It did not go smoothly. She ended up having complications when her incision became infected. She suffered miserably but still carried on like a trooper.

In early October, my mom was finally able to go back to her home with the help of home health care. She was doing better but was still not recovered from her surgery. I was able to return to work. I had been back to work for approximately ten days, when I received a call from the Arab Police Department. They were at my house and told me I needed to rush home right away. My first thought was Clint; he was home alone. They assured me that Clint was okay but they would not tell me why they were there. I had no idea what was happening, but I knew it was something bad.

CHAPTER 11

Thursday, Oct 11, 2012, when my alarm clock went off, I realized that Max was still in the bed. Normally, he had to be at work before I got up. I asked him if he was okay and he said that he was. He told me he was just a little tired and had some things that he wanted to take care of around the house, so he had decided to take the day off.

I got ready for work and, before leaving, I woke him again and reminded him that it was the day the housekeepers came. Having housekeepers was a new thing for us. My mom had contracted with them to clean our house bi-weekly. She had been using their service since dad died. When she got sick and I was missing work to take care of her, she started paying them to clean our house too, to help me out.

I said to Max, "I hate to wake you again on your day off, but it's almost 8:00, the housekeepers will be here in an hour." I teased, "If you don't want them to find you here in the bed in your undies, you probably need to get up and get dressed at least."

"That's fine. I have some things to do anyway."

"Okay, I am leaving for work. Enjoy your day. I will see you when I get home. I love you."

He said, "I love you, too. See ya after."

I went to work and quickly got caught up in the day's tasks. At 11:15am, a random thought of Max popped into my head and I picked up the phone and called his cell phone. I was just going to see how his day was going. That was unusual for me to call at that time. But the urge was strong. Max did not answer. I then called our home phone and Clint answered.

"Hey Clint, can I speak to Max, please?"

"He isn't home, Mom."

"Where is he, do you know?"

"When the housekeepers arrived. He decided to take the motorcycle out for a drive. He hasn't gotten home yet."

After we hung up, I texted Max. It was approximately 11:20am. I told him to call me when he got the message and then I texted: "Oh, by the way, be careful on that motorcycle. Clint told me you're riding."

I then went to lunch. My coworkers and I always went out and picked something up and then met in the employee break room to eat together. This day, nothing was different. I went and picked my lunch up, set my purse and phone on my desk, and headed back to the break room. We were there for about an hour. While we were eating, Mary, my friend and coworker came in through the backdoor. She was white as a sheet. She did not speak to anyone, except for David, the office manager. She told him that she needed to talk to him in his office.

I finished up the last of my lunch and headed back to my desk. I noticed that I had a voicemail on my work phone. When I listened to it, it was from the Arab police department, a message to call them. I called but they would not tell me what was wrong, just that I needed to get home right away.

My first thought was that my house was on fire and Clint was home alone. I knew this because I had just spoke to him the hour before. My adrenaline started running, my heart pounding. I went into David's office where he and Mary were still sitting. Mary was hanging up the phone. Now, they were both visibly shaken. I did not know what was going on with them.

I just blurted out, "David I hate to interrupt, but I have to go home. The police just called. I don't know what is going on, but they are at my house."

David said, "Wait, let's go into the conference room for a second. I need to talk to you."

He then guided me by the arm into the conference room. Mary followed behind. When we got in there, I could tell they knew something. I said, "Oh My God, please tell me something hasn't happened to one of my children."

He shook his head and I continued, "Is it my mom?"

"No, sweetie, I am so sorry, but it's Max. He was in a terrible automobile accident today."

"He was? Is he okay?"

He and Mary lowered their heads. "No, he's not. I am so sorry, but he's gone."

"WHAT? What do you mean he's gone?"

When the police department could not reach me, they called corporate TVA and they got a hold of Mary via cell phone. She and David were aware of what was going on and Mary immediately said that she was going to drive me to Arab. I was in shock, numb. I could not comprehend what was happening. As we were driving back, it dawned on me that Max was on his motorcycle.

"Oh My God, Mary, he was on his bike."

The rest of the trip was silent. Mary drove straight to the funeral home. There was an ambulance sitting outside.

Max had decided that morning he would ride into Huntsville and back while the housekeepers were there. It was about seventy degrees, a beautiful fall morning. He told Clint he would bring him a drink when he came home. On the way home, according to witnesses, at approximately 11:15, Max was riding seemingly fine when suddenly, without warning, he just drifted off the road into a culvert. He did not try to correct or stop the bike. No one really knows why, but I speculate that for whatever reason he lost consciousness or had a medical emergency before the crash. That is the only thing that makes sense to me. Max was forty-four years old and was an experienced biker.

Onlookers stopped to help; complete strangers started CPR on him. Witnesses told me that the rest of the people who had stopped, but could not help, formed a circle around him and joined in prayer. That brings me real comfort. The paramedics arrived and immediately continued CPR and called for Med-Flight.

Max was loaded into the ambulance and was being driven to the site for Med-flight to land when the emergency room doctor canceled the helicopter. The paramedics had been in constant communication with the doctor, they had also been doing CPR for close to half an hour at that point. They declared him deceased and the ambulance went straight to the funeral home. But since we, his family, had not authorized that specific funeral home, they had to wait with him until I arrived to say it was okay to take him inside.

After I told them they could take him inside, they made Mary and me wait. Police officers were there trying to get information from me. I was not processing what was happening well at all. Finally, they came out and said I would have to come back and identify the body and confirm that it was Max. Mary went with me. What a true friend. They then handed me two zip-lock bags with his personal belongings, which included his wallet, a pack of cigarettes, a lighter, an e-cig, six dollars and some change, his lucky money clip, and his keys.

With that we were free to go. Free to go where? I told Mary I wanted to go to my mom's house. I now had the task of telling her and kids what happened. When we walked into my mom's house, it happened that her home health care nurse, Becky, was there with her. My mom's face lit up seeing me walk in, but then it dawned on her that it was the middle of the day and that I was not okay. I told her what happened and she and I both cried. The nurse started trying to take care of us both.

I told my mom, "I have to go. I have to tell the kids."

She insisted on coming, too. My mom was not in good health. She still had drainage tubes and was using a walker. I tried to get her to stay with the nurse, but she refused.

We went home, when we pulled onto the drive, my Aunt Faye and Uncle Al and my friend Susan were already there. They had heard the news and came right away.

We all walked in. Clint said to me, "Mom, the police were here looking for you. I told them you were at work, but that Max would be home soon. They wouldn't tell me why they were here. Am I in trouble, mom?"

Oh, how my heart broke. I had to tell him and try to explain. He clearly was hurt but confused. About that time Jessica came home from school. She was ten and in fifth grade. She walked into a houseful of people and instantly said, "What is going on, why is everyone here?"

I had to tell her that her dad was gone. Despite the obviously bad situation of Max's passing, having to tell Clint and Jessica, was the hardest thing I have ever done in my life. How do you tell a ten-year-old that her dad just died? How do you explain something like that to Clint? I just remember telling them both how sorry I was. I also remember feeling like, for the first time as a mom, I could not explain why something happened or shield them enough. I could not fix this!

I know that in the next few days after Max died, we made the arrangements, had the funeral, had visitors, and made phone calls. Max's family came from Canada. My family and friends came from all over to grieve with us. I remember them being here and I do remember bits and pieces of the time, but honestly, the whole two weeks after Max died are lost to me; I do not remember much of it. My brain shut it down and shut it out.

I do know that at Max's funeral we played Bob Seger's *Turn the Page*, which is not really a conventional funeral song, but it was one of Max's favorite songs. When it started, unsolicited, everyone in the congregation, one by one, started singing it. By the middle of the song, the whole grieving auditorium was singing *Turn the Page* in Max's honor. I have never seen anything like that before. All I could think though is how cool it was and how much Max would have loved that.

Max was buried on Monday. On the following Friday, I was on the way to the airport to take Max's aunt and uncle for their flight back to Canada. On the way, I got a phone call that my mom was being transported by ambulance to Huntsville Hospital. With the events of the past week, the stress was too much for her. She was admitted into the hospital where she stayed for days. I left the airport and went straight to the hospital. I never really had time to grieve. My mom needed me, and my children needed me. They were looking to me to know what to do.

After Max died, I wanted to give up, but I did not. My friend Susan probably saved my life once or twice. She did not realize it, but I am thankful. She was one of those friends who did not just go about life after Max died. Instead, she would come into my house unannounced with dinner or with an invitation for the kids to go out for ice cream. She was also one of those people who would talk to me for hours when I felt like giving up; she kept it real. She would just tell me to get my ass up and keep going... I will be forever grateful to her.

My mom was also such a blessing. Moms have a way, don't they? She demonstrated to me how to handle the grief with grace and dignity. In the months that followed, she would be in and out of the hospital a lot. She still always smiled, never complained. There were days (between trying to balance the times I could work, being with my mom, and being a newly windowed mom with the demands of taking care of the house and getting Clint and Jessica to all of their obligations) when I thought I was going to lose my mind. It was not easy. During that time, in addition to my mom being ill, Jessica broke her arm and was also diagnosed with Asthma. She also played softball and took horseback riding lessons. Clint was still working two days a week and had to be driven and picked up. Mom, of course, had chemo, and TVA had demands as well. People were kind, truly kind. And TVA was wonderful to me. I was missing a lot of work and they had every reason to fire me, but they did not.

And even with all of this going on, I handled the rigors of most days well, at least as far getting everyone where they needed to be. When I did feel overwhelmed, I reminded myself what Susan once told me right after Max died. She said, "You cannot take on everything at once, just remember when you are eating an elephant, you cannot swallow it whole, you have to tackle it one bite at a time."

I also reminded myself of the adage: "The Lord will never give you more than you can handle; if he brings you to it, he will bring you through it."

As a result, most days, I was able to keep things in perspective, but I do remember a particular hard day. It is funny how it is never the big things that break you, but the small ones. When Jessica broke her arm, she was on our driveway riding a scooter with some friends. That happened over a weekend, so of course, the hospital could not do anything but put her in a splint and give her a sling. They made us an appointment for the following Tuesday with an orthopedic doctor in Guntersville to get her cast.

That Tuesday was also the day my mom was supposed to have a chemo treatment in Huntsville. Huntsville and Guntersville are in opposite directions from Arab. I thought back to all the friends and family who had told me if I ever needed help to just call them. I spent the whole day Monday trying to find someone who could take my mom for Chemo, but because it was such short notice, I could not find anyone who was available. It really was not personal, but it felt like it and I felt defeated. I thought *that is okay. I can do this!* My plan was to drive mom to Huntsville and drop her off and then drive to Guntersville and sit with Jessica while she got her cast, and then drive back to Arab to pick up Clint. We would all three then drive back to Huntsville and pick-up mom and find a restaurant on the way back home to eat dinner together.

I loaded everyone up in the car. Mom was sitting up front and Jessica in the back. My mom looked frail, she had no hair and was wearing a little cap on her head, and I do not know why but for some reason she kind of reminded me of a little turtle sitting there. Jessica was sitting in the back with her broken arm draped over her belly, wearing a big black sling that seemed to swallow her. I was trying to stay calm and collected, but I did worry about how my plans for the day were going to work out logistically, and I did feel a bit overwhelmed. All I do know is that the three of us were most surely a sight.

I was driving into Huntsville when I noticed blue lights in my rear-view mirror. I thought, *Are you kidding me right now?* I pulled over and a serious looking police officer approached my car and said, "Ma'am, I need your license, registration, and proof of insurance. Do you mind telling why you are in such a hurry?"

"I am sorry, officer. I didn't realize that I was speeding." I pointed towards my mom and said, "I have to take her to Crestwood for Chemo."

I then pointed at Jessica and continued, "And then get her over to Guntersville to get a cast for her broken arm."

At the same time, I handed him my registration and license but for the life of me, I could not find my insurance card. I was frantically rummaging through everything, my wallet, glove box, and console. The police officer just stood impatiently, watching. Meanwhile mom and Jessica just stared straight ahead, it was so awkward, and I felt like laughing but I knew that would be inappropriate. To break up the awkwardness (and while still rummaging), I looked at the officer and said, "Again, I am sorry, but please give me a second and I will find my insurance card." I then paused for a second before continuing, "You know, on days like today, I just sometimes wish there were two of me... But then I realize, they would just give me twice as much to do..."

With that, I saw his serious stone face change into a full chuckle. He said, "Ma'am, just quit searching for your insurance card, I believe you. And right now, you have enough to worry about without me giving you a speeding ticket; just do me a favor and slow down."

"Yes sir, and thank you."

CHAPTER 12

After Max died, Clint was a little lost. He came to me one day and told me that since Pa-pooh and Max were gone, he had been thinking and realized that he was now the man of the house. It was one of the sweetest things. He took it upon himself to do more chores around the house. He learned to wash clothes and load the dishwasher. He also took the garbage out every week. Because of his sense of routine, he did his chores without missing a beat and without ever complaining. I had not expected that of him but must admit it was a lot of help.

Clint also reached back out to his dad. It had been years, but he started calling him on the phone and talking to him. His dad asked him to lunch. Clint wanted to go, but not alone. He asked my mom to go with him. She agreed and they met at a local BBQ place, and it went well. Since Clint had last spoke to his dad, Travis had lost both of his parents and grandparents and had some health issues himself. Clint noted that his dad was different, seemed more patient and kinder somehow. I surmised that life would do that; it seems to have a way of humbling us all.

My mom continued with her chemo once a week, every week. Some weeks it was twice. She also had to go in for shots, transfusions, and blood work to try and mitigate the damage being wreaked on her body by the chemo. And while the occasion of us driving the thirty-five miles one way to Huntsville two or more times a week was a terrible thing, I would not have traded a moment of it. Obviously, I would have given anything for my mom to not be sick, but those trips are something I will treasure forever. She and I were mother and daughter, but now for the first time in my life, we were also friends, peers, and confidants. We shared in a club that not many know; we were both mothers who had watched our children's heart break at the loss of a parent. We were both widows, and we were both trying to navigate the new normal. We became bonded by strength, we talked about everything, God, dreams, fears, regrets, dying, and most importantly we talked about living. It was a profound time in my life. I learned what my mom thought about things and I think she learned a lot about me too, not just as her child but as a woman.

My mom went to either Clearview Cancer Center or Crestwood Hospital in Huntsville each week for her Chemo treatments. When one saw her at either place, one would think that she had a job as a Good Will Ambassador. She never met a stranger; she would literally talk to everyone. She freely gave out hugs and words of encouragement.

My mom and dad had a lifelong friend named Donald Davis. Donald was an author and a pastor. He lived in South Carolina and wrote faith-based columns in his local paper. He also wrote a couple of books regarding God and Cancer. These were inspiring books to help cancer patients with their illness through faith. Donald, with the help of some of his friends, had been paying to self-publish these books and provide them free of charge to any cancer survivors who wanted them.

 When mom started going to chemo, she called Donald and requested copies of his books to give out at the Cancer Institute. Each time she would requests them, she would send Donald a check to pay for them. One day, Donald called her and told her she did not have to do this. He said as part of his ministry, he was committed to giving the books away free of charge to anyone who wanted them. My mom insisted on paying, though. She told him that the more copies she paid for the more resources he would have to get the books to others. In the two years that my mom went for chemo, she paid for and gave away more than a hundred copies of his books to encourage others.

My mom also got involved in knitting for cancer patients. She learned from the other patients that there was a need to help ladies who had had mastectomies. They needed stuffing for their bras so they would look more natural. There was a call for anyone who knew how to knit to volunteer to make "knitted knockers" for these women. My mom volunteered right away and made and donated several sets to ladies who needed them.

In January 2014, TVA announced an early retirement, agency wide, for anyone wanting to take it. They were trying to reduce staff levels. My position was not the target of the cut back, but I put in my papers to retire in June. I was tired and overwhelmed and just felt that my time would be better spent with my mom and my children. But I had been at TVA for almost fifteen years, so it was a difficult decision. My mom understood it though and assured me that she thought I was doing the right thing.

I spoke to her about my desire to open my own business one day. My mom loved that idea and said that she wanted to be my partner. I think by her dreaming and planning for a future of us owning a business together gave her a new sense of hope.

In the months that followed, we talked daily about the business prospect. After much consideration, I decided that I wanted to open something "fun." I decided on an entertainment center with bowling, laser tag, arcade, and restaurant. Mom was excited. She was invested in the idea and we hired a consultant and a lawyer. Mom told all her friends that she was opening a bowling alley. However, at the same time, with each passing month my mom was getting sicker and weaker. We would have a triumph and then a setback. It was a vicious and perpetual cycle. Her body was failing her, but not her mind. She was sharp. Through it all, she kept her spirits up, never complaining, and never quitting. On the good days, she called and visited with friends, played with her dog, went out to eat. She wanted to enjoy every minute. She especially loved to spend time with Clint and Jessica, loved to bake cookies, or watch movies. She was living in the moment. She inspired many people during this time with her goodwill. Her attitude and perseverance were profoundly moving.

In some of our many discussions we talked about death and dying. We both knew what was in store for her. One day I told my mom that if there were any way for her to send me a sign from the other side that she and my dad were okay, to please do so. She assured me that if she were able to do so, she would.

My mother always maintained her faith; she stated that she was not afraid to die. One day I asked her why she fought so hard if she were not afraid to die. She explained that she was afraid to leave me. She was worried that I would not be able to handle another loss. She told me that she thought that I still needed her. Well, we always need our mothers, but that is not really what she was referring to. She was worried about me being alone, my mental health, and my ability to cope with another loss. I got it. I also realized that in the biggest struggle of her life, she was suffering and forging on because she was worried how her death would affect me. I tried to reassure her that when the time came, I would be okay, although I was not sure if that was true.

I admired my mom's faith. I always believed in God; I was steadfast in my belief. But I must admit, there were days through all this that I struggled with my faith. I really could not understand how so much suffering and loss could be placed on one family, on my family. I could not understand why a woman as wonderful as my mom could be stricken with such a terrible disease. I was never mad at God, but disappointed and hurt. We did not deserve this, my children did not, and my sweet mother did not either. When I would express my grievance towards God, my mother would have no part of it.

Her faith was unwavering. She told me that her life had been blessed. She had been married to the love of her life for over fifty years, her children were healthy, and she herself had enjoyed good health until she was old. She talked me into going to church with her. I had not been in years, but it became a refuge. Mom encouraged me to draw closer to God instead of turning away. She told me, "God knows what he is doing, you just have to trust."

You just have to trust. Being reminded of this was huge. I did just as she instructed, and she was so right.

CHAPTER 13

In January 2014, I met Matt. He was seven years older than me, very handsome, kind, and recently divorced. Matt had a demeanor unlike anyone I had ever met, very disciplined and easy going. I was instantly drawn to him because of his personality. I always felt that even though I was seemingly holding everything together, right below the surface, I was drowning a bit. And amid the chaos in my life, both externally and internally, Matt brought a calm to me that I was desperate for and had not known. I genuinely liked him. We got together a couple of times and chatted, but I would always exit quickly, so as not to make the attraction obvious.

When he asked me out the first time, I must admit, I panicked. I was excited that he was showing interest in me because I was interested in him as well, but then the realization of what my life was hit me hard, like a ton of bricks. First, I was a widow of just a little over a year. What would people think? I also was the primary caretaker of my mother, who at that point was extremely ill. I also had two kids, Clint with the challenges of his disabilities, and Jessica who had just lost her dad a little over a year ago. I was also their caretaker. I, at that time, still had a full-time job, plus a house, and a menagerie of animals to take care of it. I gave myself every excuse to say no. But I wanted to say yes.

I agreed to meet him in Huntsville for dinner. The kids stayed with my mom. I did not tell them I had a date. I figured there was no need. We went to Chili's to eat and ended up sitting there for several hours talking and laughing and getting to know each other. The time flew by. It was delightful and was the first time in a long time that I felt a little carefree.

And while I thought that I was doing a good job being discreet, Jessica was a very smart insightful twelve-year-old. Mom told me that as soon as I dropped them off, Jessica interrogated her about why I was going to Huntsville. She finally asked my mom straight up if I had a date.

The following week was my birthday. My mom, kids, and my friends, Susan and Dahlia, fixed dinner at my house and came to help me celebrate. We were taking a few photographs. I asked Jessica if she would take one of me with Susan and Dahlia. At the very moment that she had my phone to snap a picture, Matt texted me and she saw it. After everyone left, we talked. To say the least, she was not happy that Matt and I were seeing each other.

I panicked again, later that night I called Matt and instantly just started babbling, saying, "Listen, I know we haven't been seeing each other long, and I know that normally there is a time, when you first meet someone, that you play it cool, no obligations. I know it is not that deep, but I am in a different situation. I have a lot on the go, and a lot of people who are affected by my decisions right now. I just don't have time to play the dating game." I continued, "You are a good guy, you really are, but I need to stop this now, especially if you are trying to weigh out all of your dating options…. I know you are newly divorced. There is nothing wrong with that, but I just can't do it right now…"

He interrupted, "Are you done yet?'

"Yeah."

"Paula, I really like you. I know it's new. We will take it slow, but I am happy so far and I promise you I am not playing games. I really do like you."

"Really? Are you sure?" I said in disbelief.

"Yes, I am sure."

"Well, okay then."

I decided the best thing at that point was for Clint and Jessica just to meet Matt. I invited him over for dinner. He brought them each some candy. We ate dinner, made small talk, played some board games, and then retired to the living room. Awkwardly, Matt sat on the couch while Clint and Jessica, sitting across the room, just stared at him uncomfortably.

To end the awkwardness, I finally said to them, "Guys, you don't have to just sit in here. If you want to go do something else, that will be alright."

They both replied, almost in unison, "No, we're okay. We'll just stay here."

And then they both just continued to stare at Matt.

After about ten or fifteen minutes of that, Matt looked at his watch and said, "Wow guys, look at the time, I really must be going."

The next morning, Matt came and picked me up and took me out for breakfast. I told him if he was sure he wanted to continue with me, that there was one other person I wanted him to meet. We drove over to my mom's house. My mom was excited to meet Matt. I had been telling her about him since we started talking, and she had been wanting to meet him. She was gracious and he was, too. It warmed my heart how kind they were to each other. We stayed and talked with my mom for over an hour.

The following week, during our trip to Huntsville for Chemo, my mom told me that she thought Matt was nice. She said, "But I have a question: what is it about him? Why do you like him?"

"Well, I haven't really thought about it like that. It's hard to put into words, but from the first moment we started talking, it just came easy... Hmm, Mom, honestly, I am not sure exactly, but I feel like I have known him for a long time, being with him is very comforting somehow."

She interrupted, "You know why I liked him so much?

"No, why?"

"Because he reminded me of your dad, a lot."

That was it. She nailed it. That is why I liked him so much too, why it seemed so comfortable and familiar. Matt was a lot like my dad, easy going, a good listener, loved music, loved family, loved Alabama football, fishing and meatloaf, just to name a few things they had in common.

I said, "Mom, I think that you are so right." Not one to believe in a lot of coincidences, I then said, "Mom, do you think, maybe, he was heaven sent, like, maybe Dad (and Max) helped pick him and placed him on my path?"

"I don't know, could be possible."

And while we will never know, I feel comfort in thinking about it this way. I cannot help but think how much my dad would have liked Matt and I cannot help but believe that if Max couldn't be here, he would be happy to know I had such a wonderful and caring man with me, Clint and Jessica. Having said that, I must admit, Jessica was not so inclined to think the same way at first.

The next week, Matt and I went to a hockey game and took Jessica and one of her friends. Then the weekends that followed, we would do other fun things and always include Jessica and Clint. Even going camping one weekend. Matt was trying hard to get to know Jessica and he was always truly kind. But no matter what he said or did, she was unwavering in her coldness. She would respond when he spoke to her, but she was very direct and to the point, almost bordering on disrespectful.

Once, when she and I were out, Matt called. He was on speaker phone in the car and I told him Jessica was with me.

He said, "Hi, Jessica."

"Hey."

"How are you doing today, sweetheart?"

"Fine."

"How was school?"

"Fine."

This type of conversation went on for a few minutes and then we hung up. I was kind of upset with Jessica. I said, "Why are you so rude to him? He is trying so hard and has always been nice to you."

Jessica responded, "I just don't want to be nice to him!"

"Why would you say that?"

Her response was very telling and broke my heart. She said, "Mom, what if I give him a chance and get close to him. What if I start really liking him and then he breaks up with you in six months? That would just be another loss for me."

I finally understood.

I said, "Jessica, what if he doesn't break up with me in six months? What if we continue seeing each other, and he continues to be there for me and you? That would be a good thing."

"That would be good, but Mom, everybody who I ever love dies."

"Honey, I know it seems that way. But that is not true. Please do not build walls, you will deny yourself good people in your life by trying to avoid being hurt again."

The next weekend, Matt called and asked us if we wanted to have a movie night. We all agreed. Matt told Jessica she could pick out the movie and she wanted to watch a horror movie. I grimaced. I generally do not like scary movies. Matt told Jessica maybe he could talk me into it, if she would agree to let him hold my hand and put his arm around me during the show, so I would not be scared.

She said, "No, absolutely not."

He said, "Jessica, what will it take for you to ever let me to hold your mom's hand in front of you?"

"Nothing!"

"Nothing?"

She then responded sarcastically, "Well, I do want a laptop!"

I scolded, "Jessica!"

Matt said, "So according to you, I can never hold your mom's hand then?"

"I told you what it would take."

We all laughed. The next night when Matt arrived, we ate dinner and had a delightful evening. We spent a few hours together before it was time to watch the movie. As promised, Jessica got to choose, and she selected a horror flick. We popped some popcorn and put the movie in the DVD player. Just before hitting play, Matt said, "Jessica, before we start, will you please go out to my truck. There is a bag on the front seat. Will you bring it in?"

She did as he asked and walked in with a bag. Matt opened the bag to reveal a brand-new laptop. Jessica and I both just stared in shock.

I said, "Matt, what did you do?"

"It is for Jessica. She named her price. I am tired of having to sneak around to hold your hand, so, I decided to meet her demand."

That was it. From then on, Matt and I carried on a normal dating couple relationship. Every now and then if he kissed me or held my hand, she would roll her eyes and he would remind her that she had a new laptop. I must say, that was an epic move on his part, well played.

It was still a slow transition between them two, but in time, Jessica came to genuinely love Matt. Matt never pushed anything. He never wanted to overshadow her dad. But over time and consistency, he proved himself to be solid. He was truly a good guy and he was always there for her. He would take her places, paint her room, give her money to go out with her friends. Go to her events and root her on in all that she did. He taught her to drive and even after she started driving, he drove about thirty miles to Decatur to help her with a flat tire once. He never told her "no". He was always there for her no matter what, but he allowed it to be on her terms. She started referring to us as her parents. She missed her dad, but she loved Matt, too. She finally admitted to me one day that she felt lucky and blessed to have had two "dads" that both loved her.

Matt also had children and grandchildren of his own. Those relationships, between his sons and me, also proved hard to forge. Brian and Michael were grown adults with families of their own. And while they were always polite to me, they were also very distant. In the first couple of years that Matt and I dated, I generally felt excluded from their relationship because of little things, like their never asking for my phone number or sending me friend requests on Facebook. They would invite us to something occasionally, but would always go through Matt. I was included but felt that it was only as an afterthought. The invites always seemed to be for, "Their dad and, oh yeah, his girlfriend too," It was impersonal towards me and it hurt my feelings. Matt kept reassuring me that his boys had a hard time with his divorce, but they were big hearted. He kept telling me to give it time and that they would warm to me.

CHAPTER 14

Over the next few months, I continued to balance my time as I had been doing, only now with Matt in the mix. During this time, Matt was still living in Huntsville. Since his divorce, he had been in a rental house. It was also during this time that he realized that the wholesale florist business he had owned for five years was failing. He was spending a lot of time with me at my house. It was a tough time for him.

In July 2014, my mom was admitted back into the hospital. This time with pneumonia. She was extremely sick and stayed in the hospital for about ten days. During this time, they halted her Chemo and replaced it with antibiotics. When the time came for her to be released, she asked me if she could come to my house instead of going home. She did not feel like her strength was up to speed. She stayed with me for about three weeks. I took care of her. Some days were not good, but she generally seemed to be improving. When she napped, Matt and I would step out on the sun porch to talk or listen to music, so as not to disturb her. I found out later that mom was not always sleeping. She told one of her friends that she was happy I had met Matt because sometimes she would just listen to me laughing when we were outside. She told her friend she had not heard me laugh like that in over two years. I did not realize it at the time, but she was right.

Matt told me that during that time, whenever I went to the grocery store or even to the rest room, my mom would pepper him with questions about his intentions with me, asking him very pointed questions about what he liked about me, or where he saw things going, etc. I never knew it at the time but had to laugh when I found out. Even in her illness, she was my mom: always looking out for me.

In August 2014, my cousin and I hosted a family reunion for the occasion of My Uncle Quitman's 80th Birthday. My mom was feeling better and was delighted to see the entire family all together. On the last day of the reunion, my mom fell ill again and was taken by ambulance back to the hospital. By the time she arrived, she was critical and placed into ICU. The doctor on call revealed that my mom in fact did not have pneumonia as previously diagnosed. But instead, the cancer had moved into her lungs. There was nothing more they could do. He told me that I should call in the family. When I walked outside to start making the phone calls, on the ground in the parking lot, all around me, were dozens of feathers. I wondered where those came from. I told Matt, "My dad's spirit is here; he is looking after Mom and me."

The family did come, and we remained at Mom's bedside for a week, and then she improved and was upgraded from critical condition. She was released back home but this time with hospice care. My brother, Jimmy, flew in from California and the family rallied around. It truly broke my heart to see the realization in her eyes when she knew that her fight was almost over.

On the Sunday night after she went home, Mom slipped into a coma. Jimmy and I stayed with her all day on Monday. We were told she could stay in a coma for days. So, that Monday night I went home and told Jimmy to call me if there were any changes, if not, I would return first thing Tuesday morning.

When I arrived back the next morning, I walked into her house and my mom yelled out with a cheerful, "Hello!"

Jimmy told me that she awoke from the coma at about 3am and requested a bowl of ice cream.

I went to her bedside and said, "Hey Mom, I really missed you yesterday. Where were you?"

I still get chills remembering when she said, "Heaven was beautiful."

"It was? What did you see? Did you see Dad?"

"No, I didn't see Dad, but I saw beautiful trees, and then I was led to a birthday party. Someone was turning twelve. I saw twelve candles on a cake." She continued, "Then someone told me that it wasn't my time yet, they weren't quite ready for me."

From that point on, my mom was at peace, a peace I cannot describe honestly. She spent her days eating a lot of ice cream, watching her favorite programs, and visiting with family and friends. She made a point to say her personal goodbyes to each one and told them how much she loved them. There were no words left unsaid and no regrets left on the table.

My brother stayed at my mom's house until Wednesday, but then had to return home to California to handle some things there. Matt and I went to Mom's house every single day. On Thursday, August 28, we were there until around dinner time and then came home. We got into bed about midnight and the phone rang. Mom's nighttime sitter called and told me that the power was out, and she did not know how to switch Mom from the electric oxygen tank to the portable tank.

"What?"

I told her I was on my way.

In the meantime, she also called the day shift home health nurse, Pamala. Pamela tried to talk her through it on the phone but at the same time, she had jumped into her car and headed that way. She knew that my mom could not go for a long period of time without oxygen. Pamala and I both arrived at my mom's house within moments of each other. The house was completely dark. We worked together to get her back on oxygen. Something told me to stay.

I asked, "Mom, you want me to make us some coffee?"

"I would like that, but the power is out."

I reminded her that with her Bunn coffee maker, the water in the reservoir stayed hot for a while. And that I would be glad to make us some. She and I drank our coffee and talked some and even shared a few laughs. Mom was worried that it was getting late, but I assured her I was not leaving her until the power came back on and I did not. The power was not restored until 3:00 am. I got her hooked back to the permanent oxygen machine and then told her that I was going to go home, but that I would be back later in the morning. She told me to be careful going home and then she said, "I love you, very much."

"I love you very much too, Mom."

Three hours later, at 6:00 am, my phone rang. It was Pamala; she said my mother had slipped back into a coma and her vital signs were indicative that the end was near. Matt and I arrived and spent the whole day with her. I authorized Pamala to start Morphine so that my mom would not suffer in pain. We sat with her all day.

At 8:55 pm, my mom took her last breath. I was sitting right beside her on the bed, holding her hand. I had fulfilled my promise. I had been with her through the entire journey. A journey that had begun exactly three years and one month before with my dad's passing. At the very moment my mom died, the old gospel hymn, *Swing Low, Sweet Chariot*, played on the television in the background. I think it was on an abused animal commercial, I am not sure. But ironically, that was the very song my mom used to sing to me when I was a little girl. Some may say that it was just a coincidence, but I felt her spirit surround me.

After mom passed, hospice was called in to pronounce the death. Pamala stayed with us until the hospice lady arrived. Transport was called to take my mom's body to the funeral home, but because it was after hours, it was going to take an hour or more for them to get there. Shortly after Pamala left, the lady from Hospice received a family emergency phone call and had to leave unexpectedly too. So, there we were just Me, Matt, and Mom.

Matt and I sat there in solemn silence waiting for the coroner to arrive when I remembered something. I said, "Matt, how many candles did mom say was on the cake when she was in heaven?"

"Twelve. She was very specific. She said she thought that it was someone's twelfth birthday, why?"

"Oh my God, Matt, that was twelve days ago. She said they were not ready for her yet, twelve days ago, that cake was hers!"

My brother flew back from California and we planned Mom's funeral for the following Monday. The funeral was nice. My mom had already done most of the work for us, including picking out the songs she wanted played: *Amazing Grace, Just as I am*, and *Sweet Beulah Land*. I also had them play *Swing Low, Sweet Chariot*. They played that one last as they led my mom out of the chapel to her final resting place.

The day after the funeral, my brother, his girlfriend, Lori, Clint, Matt, and I were sitting in the living room at my house, talking, when suddenly the overhead ceiling fan light came on. We all froze. My brother said, "That light just turned on by itself."

Matt looked at me in disbelief and said, "Remember you told your mom to send a sign that she was okay if she could." He then looked up towards the sky and said, "Ok, mom, if that is you, we got it, you can turn the light back off."

Five seconds later, the light went off. That had never happened before and has not happened since. I fully believe that was my mom sending a sign from God to let me know that she was finally okay, at peace, and not sick anymore.

CHAPTER 15

The week after my mom's funeral, I went to her bank to close her accounts and handle some of her affairs. When I got there, the Bank President asked me what I planned to do with my mom's house. I told him that eventually my brother and I would be selling it. He told me that he knew of someone that was looking for a house and thought mom's house would be perfect. He asked if I would be willing to show it to him. It caught me off guard, but I said that I would.

Sure enough, the next day his friend, a preacher named Clint, who was moving to Arab from Mobile, called and then came to see Mom's house. He made an offer on the spot. Jimmy and I talked about it and decided that it was better to accept an offer sooner, than to wait to take the chance that we might not get another offer on Mom's house for a while. I kind of felt like it was a sign anyway, after all, the buyer was from Mobile, where my parents were originally from, he was preacher, and his name was Clint.

Preacher Clint wanted to close and move in on the first day of October. That gave us just three weeks to clear out the house. By this time, Jimmy was back in California. I struggled really, I was exhausted and was not really prepared physically or mentally to go through Mom's and Dad's stuff yet. Matt willingly helped. We boxed up things, held yard sales, gave away things, and brought things to my house. It was overwhelming really. I could not have done any of it without Matt; he was a rock. He and I continued to grow closer.

Matt was going through a tough time, too, as months earlier, he had had to close his business in Huntsville. Instead of continuing to rent, I asked if he wanted to move in with me, and he did.

It was a fast-paced time. I became very reflective. When Mom died, unlike when my dad and Max died, I did not fall into depression. My feelings were more of a resolve. It is hard to explain. I had just lost my mom, and no greater love exists, but she and I had come full circle. There were no words left unsaid and I knew how much my mom had suffered; I just felt like her job here on earth was finished. I missed her terribly, but over the past couple of years, I had prepared myself as much as I could be for her passing.

I think my soul did kind of give up a little, though. That overwhelming realization, that as much as I wanted, I really had absolutely no control over what happens in life. But for the first time ever, I was okay with that. I just laughed a little more and loved a little deeper. I wanted to be a good example for Clint and Jessica, and I did not want to waste my time on needless drama. It is a cliché, but life really is too short. By living in that reality, my outlook profoundly changed on everything.

In the fall, Matt and I and the kids felt the need for a change of scenery, a chance to recharge a little. We took a cruise to Mexico. It was a good get-away. Matt knew that one of my bucket lists items had always been to swim with dolphins. He saw to it that I got to do that. It was a great trip. Matt was so good to me. During that year, we celebrated our first Christmas together, and birthdays. The year flew by. In January, Matt and I celebrated our first anniversary together. And while our first year had been tough because of his business failure, my mom's death, and us trying to blend our families, I could not remember a time feeling happier or more hopeful. Through it all, we leaned on each other, laughed, shared... I relied on Matt and realized that I was in love with him, without doubt.

It was about this time that Matt first asked me to marry him. But when he did, I said no. I am not sure why I said no, but I just knew I was not ready. The past four years had changed me. And although I genuinely loved Matt and he and I were living together, I did not want to be attached enough to anyone or anything to get hurt again. I wanted independence. I wanted to feel like I had an escape route, I also felt like I needed time to forge a better relationship with his grown kids and grandkids. I just felt like us getting married before they had accepted me was wrong. And yet, I really had no reason to know if they ever would. It was just an excuse, I suppose. I think it hurt Matt that I said no, but he did not let on that it did. He maintained that the proposal was an open offer, whenever I was ready. He was understanding, patient, and he just continued to love me, despite myself.

For the first time in my life, I also had spare time. I was retired and my caretaker services were no longer needed. Matt was looking for work, but for a couple of months, neither of us were working. We spent time together at the pool, late nights of music, and board games. I was able to attend all of Jessica's activities and was home during the day. We became the hangout to her and her friends. It was nice, well at least for a while. But then it got old. I felt that my life had no real direction. I was not accomplishing much, and I had to figure out what to do next.

Matt took a job in management with a fast-food chain. It did him good to get back into the work force, but the job was over an hour away, so it was two hours of travel every day and then he worked for about ten. That changed our time together, and not only was he gone for twelve hard hours a day, when he got home, he was exhausted. I felt bad for him.

I put a lot of renewed thought into pursuing the opening of the business that Mom and I had dreamt of. Maybe it was time, but more than a year had passed since she and I first started; and I was afraid. In theory, it seemed like a good idea, but I had never worked for myself before. I was not sure if I knew enough about owning a business to do it. Matt encouraged me to give it a try.

I went into the venture, full throttle. I reconnected with the consultant and we started looking for buildings and financing. I had a budget but did not want to finance the entire thing by myself.

At the same time, Matt was struggling with his job. The long days were wreaking havoc on his health. He started having severe back issues from being on his feet on concrete floors for so many hours. I encouraged him to quit his job and come and work for me. It became all-consuming for the both of us. There was setback after setback with finding a building, hiring contractors, and permits. The biggest setback came from the inability to secure additional financing. I had seed money and good credit, but my business was a startup, and no bank would take a chance on me. That should have discouraged me, but the more roadblocks that were put in my way, the more determined I was to move forward. I just felt like it was something I needed to do, to prove to myself that I could. I believed in myself despite my inability to get a bank to believe in me.

I scaled back the project and decided to leave the bowling alley portion out of it. I moved forward with the arcade, laser tag and restaurant. We found a building to rent in September 2015 and started construction.

I learned so much, some of it the hard way. Construction costs overran the budget, something that I have heard is frequently the case. Companies would not meet deadlines for deliveries. So, what was supposed to have taken three months to complete took four and a half. And I spent more money than I had anticipated, but, finally, at the end of January 2016, we were ready to open.

I decided to call my business The Funky Feather. I named it that as a reminder to myself that my dad's spirit would always be with me. I also think that, more than anyone, my dad would have been the proudest of the risk and the journey I was taking. He was always an entrepreneur at heart.

I designed the logo myself, I learned to build a webpage, learned to run a restaurant, a laser tag arena, to be an accountant and I learned to manage people and projects. It was not always a smooth process; many lessons were costly. I learned that many things go into owning and operating a business. I was not always sure that I could do it, but I did learn and adapt quickly. I found strengths I didn't' know I had. I also learned when to outsource and delegate, another important factor in being a manager. You do not have to know how to do everything, but you do need to know who to call when you are in over your head.

In the end, the product was good. I loved what we had built. The Funky Feather was eclectic, different, funky, but most of all inviting and fun. It was a place where a lot of happy memories could be made. I assumed that the consultant's business plan and anticipated sale calculations were a certainty. I believed that when we built it, the crowds would come. But that did not happen right away. We initially opened to a good crowd; we were new. We had good reviews. We were on our way. But then summer came and we found out unexpectedly that our business was somewhat seasonal. People do not play as much laser tag and eat out when they can grill out and swim. Beaches are hard to compete with. Then after summer there was high school and college football season, still slow and very painful. Another hard lesson. We also were behind the curve to other businesses that already had a following of loyal customers. That would eventually come for us too, but not in the first couple of years. There were so many times during that time that I thought about giving up, but I was too stubborn to do so.

I never went anywhere, from the bank to the grocery store, that I was not an ambassador for the Funky Feather. I invited and told everyone that would listen to me about it. And, when customers did come, it was my commitment to give great customer service and great product every time. If we messed up, we would admit to it and fix it. We treated everyone who came through the door as family. It took time, but slowly it happened. We did build up a customer base which really became like family to us. We genuinely loved seeing them come in. This was by far the best part of owning my own business. We made so many friends, we saw people get married, have babies, kids grow up, and sometimes a customer face illness or death. We celebrated and mourned with them all. We invested in the community, sponsored kids sporting programs, and raised money in many of the charitable events we hosted. Our customers also came to know us and our family. Clint and Jessica spent many hours with us at the restaurant.

Clint continued to talk to his dad. He came to me one day and said that he wanted to invite his dad out to eat and to see the Funky Feather, but he did not want to be by himself. He reminded me that the last time they went out, my mom had gone with them. I did not understand his nervousness. I tried to reassure him that it would be okay to go by himself with his dad, and I also pointed out that I could not take Mom's place, as it would be awkward for his dad and for me. Matt spoke up and told that Clint if he wanted, he would be glad to sit with them. And he did. It was a great lunch for them, and it helped Clint and his dad further rebuild their relationship. It also consolidated the trust between Matt and Clint, as well as made me love Matt just a little more.

CHAPTER 16

B y 2016, we were into a routine. My relationship with Matt was going great. Clint was still working at the grocery store; at this point for seven years. And Jessica was in high school. I finally got to know Matt's sons, Michael and Brian, and their families, better. I really liked them. Matt's oldest son, Brian, and his wife, Brittney, both work in sales. They were very dynamic, warm, and energetic, and I found them extremely easy to talk to. They had three kids, Matt's grandkids, Rachel, Grant, and Carly, who I instantly fell in love with. Matt's younger son, Michael is a mini-Matt. I swear they are the same person. He and his wife, Desiree, welcomed me, and we spent a lot of time with them, hanging out, listening to music, or playing games. I loved having a big family again, especially during the holidays and the grandkids were truly a breath of fresh air. All was going well.

One evening, I was sitting outside on our back screened in porch watching TV. Matt and the kids were inside, I wondered what they were doing but was too lazy to go in and see. Then Matt walked out, and as I turned to speak to him, he instantly dropped down on one knee and opened a box containing a beautiful blue diamond engagement ring. He told me that he had talked to all the kids already and they approved, he also told me that Jessica had helped pick out my ring. He asked again if I would marry him. This time, without hesitation, I said yes.

We were married on July 3, 2016, in our backyard. A small intimate affair with just family and close friends. Clint, once again, walked me down the aisle. Jessica and two of her friends played the music for our ceremony and then Jessica took her place beside me as my maid of honor. The wedding was simple, but perfect. Afterwards, we had a cookout and a pool party with our friends. It had been such a long and painful path to get to this point, but after dating for over two and half years, I was married to my best friend.

Not long after our wedding, Matt and I realized that I could not continue to keep him on the payroll at the Funky Feather, or at least it could not be his only source of income. He would need to find another job to cover us during the slow weeks. He started applying to places, and got offered a job at the Arab Senior Center. A steady full-time job, with insurance. It was a godsend to us.

As for the Funky Feather, things were growing and doing better, but it was still a go-slow process. Matt and I did not want to give up. I did not want to fail. But we were going to have to keep winning customers over with each interaction and, if we had to, one belly at a time. That kind of became our motto. We realized that growing a business was going to take a lot more time than we anticipated. With Matt having another job, it did take some pressure off, but the downside was that he was working two jobs; one during the day and then coming to help me every evening and during the weekends. He always did so without complaint.

CHAPTER 17

In April 2018, I had a group approach me about doing a charity event at The Funky Feather. I was glad to be a part of it. The event started at 9:00am. I told Matt that I would open the restaurant and he could come in at 4:00, after he picked Clint up from work. That was exactly what he did: he picked Clint up and dropped him off at the house and then came to work. Matt and I were both at The Funky Feather for probably about an hour before I left. As I got into the car to go home, my phone rang. It was the Arab Police department letting me know they were at my house and I needed to come home. *Oh, Dear God*, I have only had the police at my house one other time and that was six years before, when they came to notify me that Max had died. I could not imagine what was happening, but I was scared all the way home.

When I got to my house there were two police cars in my driveway. I had to pull into the yard to park my car. As I got out the car, one of the officers approached me.

I asked, "What is going on, Officer?"

"We got a phone call that there was a naked man wondering around in your yard."

"What?"

The officer continued, "Yes, ma'am, and when we pulled into your driveway, the man tried to go inside house. But we restrained him before he could go inside."

I just looked at him in shock.

He continued, "Ma'am, it was Clint."

"Clint? You mean my Clint?"

"Yes Ma'am, is Clint autistic?"

I said, "No, he has some cognitive disabilities, but he is not autistic."

"We put cuffs on him, but then he started to cry and ask for his mom. We realized that something was not right. We have him sitting in the garage, but you do know we could arrest him for public lewdness and resisting. We have decided not to…not this time."

I was confused and angry, what was Clint doing? I stormed into the garage with the police officer in tow. When I got into the garage another officer was standing over Clint, who was sitting in a lawn chair, covered in a blanket.

I went right over to him with my voice raised a little, and said, "Clint! What were you thinking? You know better!"

Nervously, he responded, "I don't know, I don't know, let's just drop it. I won't ever do it again."

That is all it took for me to realize something was wrong. Clint was acting confused and was very defensive. He was also hurt. When the police cuffed him, his elbows and wrists got scraped and bruised.

I looked at the officer and said, "Officer, something isn't right. Clint is not a deviant; he is a good boy, always has been. Something is wrong, very wrong."

"Well, if you feel that way, ma'am, maybe you should have him checked out. But just realize, if we have to come back out here again, he will be going to jail."

I muttered somewhat dismissively, "Yeah, okay."

With that, they got into their patrol cars and left. I told Clint to go inside and get dressed and then get into my car. I took him straight to the emergency room. I called Matt on the way. He had the same reaction as me. In fact, when I first told him what had happened, he did not believe me. He thought that I was joking but then quickly concurred with my position that something was wrong; Clint would not have normally ever done that.

After we had been sitting in the waiting room of the hospital for about forty-five minutes, I noticed that Clint seemed to be more like himself again. I calmly asked him, "Clint honey, why were you in the yard without your clothes on? What were you thinking?"

"Mom, honestly, I don't remember doing that."

"You don't remember doing that?"

He continued, "No, I don't remember doing that. I just remember Matt dropping me off from work and I went in to get a shower, I remember getting out of the shower and I was about to get my deodorant to put on. The next thing I remember was trying to go into the house because I realized I was outside naked and I didn't want anyone to see me, but then the policemen threw me down to the ground."

We waited for a long time for Clint to be called back to triage. I informed them that I was Clint's Court appointed legal guardian as well as his mom. That designation was assigned to me after Clint became an adult. In other words, I have the legal authority to act on his behalf. I then told them everything that had happened. They took his blood pressure, temperature, and drew blood. We were then taken to a room to await the doctor.

When the doctor finally came in, I ask him about the blood work: had it shown anything? I also asked him what he thought could be wrong. He said that they were just doing a general blood profile, but mostly they were testing Clint for drugs and alcohol. He was still waiting for the results. I informed him that neither Clint nor I did drugs. I then ask him if it were possible that Clint could have had a stroke or a seizure of some sort. The doctor replied definitively, "No, neither of those would cause this kind of behavior."

After the blood results came back, the doctor returned to the room and stated that all the blood work looked good, and that Clint had tested negative for drugs and alcohol. He then said he believed that, in the absence of drugs, the only other possible explanation of Clint's condition was that he must be mentally ill or must have had some sort of psychotic episode. I told him that while Clint was mentally disabled, he was not mentally ill. I emphatically expressed to the doctor that, as Clint's caretaker, I could assure him that Clint's behavior that night was completely out of character and that I knew something was wrong, something was seriously wrong.

He refuted me by saying, "Sometimes adults with disabilities can become mentally ill, and especially in cases where we do not know their history, like for instance," he said, "his mother may have used Meth while she was pregnant, or he could have been abused as a child and it is just now manifesting."

Now I was getting mad and reminded the doctor that I was, in fact, Clint's mother and could assure him that I had never done any drugs or abused my son. He apologized, saying he heard me say that I was his legal guardian, but he did not realize that I was also his mother. He left the room and I never saw him again.

The next person that came in was a hospital social worker that the doctor had sent in to talk to Clint. She asked him for permission to talk in front of me. Again, did they not realize what me being his legal guardian meant? He is not capable of making those decisions. She should have asked me if she could talk to him. But none the less, Clint said she could ask him questions in front of me, so I let it go.

She proceeded to ask Clint a lot of questions, including if he was feeling suicidal or felt like hurting anyone, all to which he answered in the negative. She then stated that she would be authorizing his release home with me.

I asked, "Authorizing his release home with me? As opposed to what? What do you mean that you will authorize him to go home with me?"

"By law, I can have him involuntarily admitted into the hospital for seventy-two hours for observation, if I feel that he is a danger to himself or others, but since I don't feel that he is, I am going to let him go home with you."

A discharge nurse then came in with a list of area mental health professionals and their phone numbers along with a discharge paper with the diagnosis of "acute psychosis" attached. She advised that we follow up with a psychologist or psychiatrist.

When we left the hospital, I felt completely humiliated and dismissed. The only substantive thing they did in the four hours we were there was to give Clint a completely unnecessary drug test. Afterward, they treated Clint like he was crazy, and me, like I was possibly an abuser.

On the following Monday, I called Clint's General Practitioner to make an appointment. It took approximately ten days before they could get him in to be seen. When I told the doctor what had happened, he immediately ordered a CT scan. The very next day, his office called me to let me know that the scan results were in and they saw something that was concerning. They then ordered an MRI and EEG. It took a couple of days to get that set up.

After those results came back, we received the diagnosis Arteriovenous

Malformation (AVM) on the right partial lobe of his brain. An AVM is an abnormal connection between arteries and veins, basically an area where the high-pressure arteries feed directly into low pressure veins bypassing the capillary system. The concern with such a condition is the real possibility of a brain bleed. A brain bleed can cause irreparable damage or death. Clint was born with this condition, but it was never discovered and because it was asymptomatic, we did not know about it. That is until the day Clint was found wandering outside. As I found out, seizures are a tell-tale symptom of a worsening AVM. Additionally, it was confirmed that Clint was actively having a Complex Partial Seizure the night we went to the Emergency Room. And when the EEG was done almost two weeks later, Clint was still having continual mild conscious active seizures.

The thought still frightens me that the night we went to the emergency room, Clint was having an active seizure in real time. As I learned later, one of the classic symptoms of this type of seizure is a loss of memory and wandering. Because the local hospital did not take it seriously, two valuable weeks were lost. And had I not taken the initiative and followed up with someone else, we may not have found the AVM in time. I still cannot fathom why at the very least they did not order a simple CT scan that night. I could go on, but it was truly scary to think of all the what if's.

After the diagnosis, Clint was immediately put-on anti-seizure medication and referred to a neurologist in Huntsville. The neurologist in Huntsville then subsequently referred him to a neurosurgeon at The University of Alabama Hospital (UAB) in Birmingham. An AVM is quite a serious condition. It affects only about two percent of the population. To our good fortune, Birmingham is one of the hospitals in the country with doctors who specialize in the treatment of AVM's.

Clint's neurosurgeon was Dr. Stetler. My first impression of him was that he seemed young for a neurosurgeon, probably in his forties, just finishing his internship perhaps. He was apparently smart, engaged, and efficient. He ordered several more tests and scans and angiograms. Clint handled everything well, even though I knew that he was scared. I think on some level he was also relieved to be getting help. With the mini seizures that he had been having, he was also having mild headaches and trouble concentrating. But he was unable to articulate to us what he was feeling. We had noticed Clint occasionally staring off into space or losing concentration, but we had just attributed it to his disabilities. I feel terrible that we did not realize sooner the distress he was in.

It also occurred to me, that the AVM was most possibly the source of his disabilities. For all these years, we never had a reason, but now maybe this was the answer. The other thing that flashed into my mind was the conversation with my dad the months before he died, the conversation in which he expressed that he thought that we were missing something and should have Clint rechecked. I wish I had heeded that advice. I also wish that my dad was still here, and I could tell him that he was so right.

After many months of consultations and several evaluations, Dr. Stetler told us that the AVM had to be removed, if not, he was most certain that within a matter of time, it would cause a stroke, brain bleed, or death. He also determined that while the AVM was not inoperable, it was deep enough into the brain that he was concerned that operating would be too risky, without a guaranteed safe result. He believed that the best course of treatment instead would-be radiation surgery. He brought aboard another specialist; a radiologist named Dr. Doublebower.

The way the procedure was explained to me was that they would map the very precise location of the AVM in the brain and zap it with one extremely high dose of radiation. The radiation would burn the AVM (similar to a sunburn) causing the body to divert function from that area while it tried to heal. Then over time, scar tissue would form, and the body would just reject the AVM altogether, and it would shrink away. This is a very elementary explanation. The medical procedure itself is obviously more complex than explained, but it is the best way I can explain it for it to make sense.

The doctors said that the success of the surgery could take up to two years to fully realize as the body's way of processing the radiation was a slow one. There should be no real sides effects from the surgery itself, but during the two-year process, Clint would still be at the same risks of having a brain bleed as he was before radiation, until the AVM was gone. They felt that it was still the best course of action. We were all just praying that radiation would work before something worse happened.

They told us that if Clint were to have a brain bleed while we were home, the symptoms would be a headache like no other. They assured me that if that happened, I would know it was not just a normal headache. They told me that if there were any indication of a brain bleed or stroke, I would need to get Clint to Birmingham as quickly as possible. Scary stuff, but I agreed and signed the authorization for the radiation surgery. It was set to take place in October of 2018, six months after the initial diagnosis.

I must say that I was very impressed with Dr. Stetler and Dr. Double-bower. Both were deeply knowledgeable in their field and they worked well together managing Clint's case. They were also both good at explaining things to us and answering questions. I never felt dismissed or uninformed.

Clint had the surgery at the oncology hospital in Birmingham. Afterward he was very tired for a few days, but he never had any other noticeable side effects. In the months that followed, we went back and forth to Birmingham for follow ups, MRI's and consultations with both doctors every three months to track the progress of the radiation. In the meantime, we were told that unless there was a problem, Clint could resume life as normal.

By May of 2019, it had been seven months since Clint's surgery. Everything seemed to be moving along nicely. Clint was back at work with no side effects. We had already had two follow-ups with the doctors. The MRI that he had in May showed a little bit of swelling around the AVM site but no change to the AVM itself. Dr. Stetler said that was exactly what they would expect. He said the swelling showed that the radiation had pinpointed the right spot and the fact that the AVM had not started shrinking yet was also normal as well. He reminded us that it could take up to two years and was a slow process. He said slow change was best. He felt that it was possible by the time we returned for the next MRI, in August, we may start seeing a little change in the AVM, although even then he did not expect much change yet either. He assured that everything was going just as he expected.

During that meeting, Dr. Stetler also informed us that he had decided to join a practice in his hometown in North Carolina. He would be leaving Birmingham. He said that he would be referring Clint to another neurosurgeon within the practice in Birmingham for future follow-ups. We hated that, we had grown to really rely on and trust him.

For Clint's next visit, Dr. Stetler told us that Clint would be seeing Dr. Fisher. We found out later that Dr. Fisher was not only another

Neurosurgeon in that practice; he was the head of the Neurosurgery Department and was also a Professor of Neurosurgery at the college. He taught future neurosurgeons how to be neurosurgeons. He was also ranked as one of the top neurosurgeons in the entire country.

CHAPTER 18

In the summer of 2019, I started actively looking for a job. Matt was already working two jobs. I decided to go back to work as well. The Funky Feather was holding its own, but I was not making a consistent salary. Jessica was about to start her senior year of high school and with all the imminent expenses, I felt that the extra income would be helpful.

In July, I was offered a job in the Probate office at the courthouse. It seemed to be the perfect fit for what I was trying to accomplish. It was a typical Monday through Friday business hours job, which gave me the opportunity to still be fully engaged with The Funky Feather during the evenings and weekends. It was a tough transition working for someone else again, getting up early, working two jobs, etc., but I enjoyed the challenge. I learned quickly and was picking up the task of the new job well.

In August, just about a month and a half after starting my new job, I woke up in the middle of the night with the worst diarrhea and stomach pain I have ever had. It was so bad I had to call in sick. I felt bad because I knew how it looked to miss work so quickly after starting. I could not help it though; I was sick. I felt so bad that I needed to see a doctor. I also thought that if I went to the doctor, I would at least have a doctor's note and be able to prove that I was not lying. It is weird how my brain works, but I guess that is the employer in me. As an employee, I was more worried about how it looked or if they believed me than I was about how sick I really felt. My doctor checked me out, and said I had a bad stomach virus and if given a couple of days, he felt that it would run its course. He said I could return to work as soon as I felt able.

By the next day, the diarrhea had subsided. I did not have a temperature, but the stomach pain was still intense. I felt terrible. I could not eat anything. But I got up and headed back to work, and apologized profusely for my absence. My stomach continued to hurt, yet I worked through the pain for three or four days. I kept just thinking that eventually the virus would run its course and I would get well, but I did not.

The pain and loss of appetite just kept getting worse. By the beginning of the week, I called Matt from work in tears and told him that when I got off, I was going to go back to the doctor to see if there was anything he could give me.

I worked the rest of the day. By the time I got home my regular doctor's office was closed, so I went to an Urgent Care Clinic. After an exam at the clinic, they told me that I needed to go straight to the emergency room. They did not have a CT scan machine at the clinic but felt that I needed a more depth examination than they were capable of. I was upset, mainly because I had just spent two hours there. I did not feel well and now it was already close to eight pm. I told Matt, "I have to work tomorrow, we just wasted all of this time at the clinic and now I am going to spend the rest of the night at the ER, that's not happening! Let's just forget it and go home."

But Matt would not let me do that; he insisted that we go on to the emergency room to get me checked out. We were in the waiting room for twenty or thirty minutes, before they called me into triage. Once in triage, they took my temperature. It was over 102 degrees. I was taken for a CT scan immediately. The doctor came in and informed us that I had a severe case of diverticulitis, an infection of my colon. I was extremely sick, apparently pushing through for a week had not been the right thing to do. The infection was now bad enough that the doctor stated that I was going to be admitted into the hospital.

I spent the next three days in the hospital on a liquid diet and IV antibiotics. When I was discharged, I was sent home with more strong antibiotics. Between the infection and the antibiotics, the diarrhea returned. I was on the road to getting better, though I still felt terrible, but once again, I returned to work.

At this same time, Clint started complaining that he had a headache. When I ask him how bad it was, he said mild. I gave him Tylenol. I was concerned because of his surgery, but the doctors in Birmingham had told me that it was possible for him to have headaches occasionally. They warned that if he had a severe headache, we should get him back there quickly, but they also assured me that I would know the kind of headache they were referring to. If it happened, they said Clint would not be able to function, and it would be obvious. For anything less, just treat with Tylenol, so that is what we did.

Clint's headache continued for several days. But with each dose of Tylenol, he said he felt like it was helping. I could tell he did not feel well, but it did not seem to be anything to be overly concerned about. One day, while I was at work, Matt called and told me that Clint had just thrown up what looked to be phlegm. He told me he was going to take him to the doctor and just have him checked out. We both surmised that with the headaches and now vomiting, he probably had a sinus infection. That is exactly what the doctor confirmed. He gave Clint a steroid shot and some antibiotics. After the shot, Clint seemed better.

The next day, I went to work again. It had been exactly one week since I was discharged from the hospital. I called and checked on Clint several times during the day. He said that he felt better, but his head was still hurting a little. I told him that we needed to give the antibiotics a couple of days to kick in. I suggested that he just take it easy and rest.

When I got home that night, we were settling in for the evening. Matt and I were relaxing when Clint came into the living room. He said something nonsensical and pointed to his mouth. I said, "What did you say, Clint?"

He said it again, and it was just garble. Clint nervously laughed. Matt and I looked at each other and both knew that something was amiss. Matt said, "Clint, do me a favor and say your ABCs."

"A B C D E K Z…"

"Count to ten," Matt said.

"A B C D G…"

Matt continued, "Clint, what are the names of our dogs?"

"I am not sure."

"Who is your sister?"

"I don't know."

Clint then started getting really frustrated. A tear ran down his check. He told me his head was hurting again and he just wanted to go and lie down. I told him that he could not do that. I was going to call an ambulance and get him checked out.

I called 911 and tried to explain to dispatch what was going on and his condition. The paramedics arrived. They were very attentive and nice, but I do not think they understood the seriousness of the AVM. Clint was still confused and unable to answer simple questions, but all his vital signs were good. The paramedics said they would go ahead and take him to the hospital but assured me that with his vitals being good, they felt like it was not anything to be overly worried about.

They ask me if I wanted him to go to our local hospital or if I would prefer, he could be transferred to Huntsville. I said Huntsville. They told me I could ride with him in the ambulance and Matt could follow. Once in the ambulance, I was told to sit in the passenger seat. Clint was in the back with a paramedic. They never turned on the sirens or lights, although later, Matt told me that they were flying, and he had a hard time keeping up with them. But I did not realize that at the time. The driver was making small talk with me all the way and the lights were not on, so I remember thinking that maybe I should not have called the ambulance, maybe we should have just called the doctor and taken him ourselves.

The paramedic in the back would occasionally step-up front to ask me a question. Once she asked me how old Clint was. She said she had asked him, but he told her that he was ninety-two. She joked that she did not think that could be right. Other than that, she told me that his vitals were still good, and the rest of his conversation seemed to be lucid. He did not seem to be confused with his answers as much as he was when they got to the house. Again, I was thinking to myself, perhaps I jumped the gun calling them and requesting a trip to Huntsville.

The driver remained calm the whole trip. He kept me calm. But unbeknownst to me, the paramedic in the back was communicating with the ER doctor in Huntsville the entire way. As soon as we arrived at Huntsville, Clint was taken straight from the ambulance into the trauma unit, doctors and nurses were standing in the bay waiting on us. There was a flurry of activity.

I had the paperwork from Birmingham and was able to explain to them that he had an AVM that was already being treated with radiation. The emergency room doctor in Huntsville was amazing, and the nurses too. As soon as we got into the room, Clint started crying. He kept saying his head was hurting really bad and then he threw up again. The doctor wasted no time sending Clint for an MRI STAT. They could not really give Clint anything until the results were in, but eventually did give him something for pain and nausea.

Just like always at the hospital, it took hours to get any answers. Clint had dozed off and Matt and I just waited. The doctor finally came back in and said that the MRI showed a severe amount of swelling in his brain around the AVM site. He stated that was the cause of the confusion and headache and the severity of the headache was causing the vomiting. He stated that they had already called UAB and talked to the neurologist on call there. They had decided it would be best for Clint to be in Birmingham where his surgeon was. By now, it was already about 1am in the morning. I asked, "Should we drive him there?"

The doctor said, "No, we are going to be transporting him by ambulance."

"When?"

"Tonight, as soon as we can get one over. It may still be an hour or so, but we are going to go ahead and transport him as soon as possible," he continued, "I am also going to assign a nurse to ride with him, just to be on the safe side."

When the doctor left the room, Matt and I decided that if I could go with Clint in the ambulance, he would go to the house and check on Jessica and make sure she was up in time for school, he would grab an overnight bag for me and my phone charger.

The ER doctor in Huntsville had started Clint on steroids, which helps with swelling. They were taking good care of him, but they seemed kind of nonchalant. There was a plan to send him to Birmingham. Other than that, no one seemed overly urgent, everyone was calm.

The paramedics arrived around two thirty in the morning. They said I could ride with them, so, Matt kissed me goodbye and said he would go back to Arab, handle a few things, and then drive down to Birmingham. He said he would see me in a few hours, then he left. The paramedics loaded Clint into the ambulance and a nurse appeared and introduced herself. I saw her badge; she was a critical care nurse. She was who we had been waiting on. Her job was strictly to ride with patients that needed care during transport. It was not until that moment that I figured out that Clint was sicker than I realized.

When we arrived in Birmingham, the doctors and nurses again were actively waiting for us. They were communicating with the critical care nurse all the way there and knew exactly the moment we pulled in. They took Clint directly to Neurological ICU and the staff started working on him fervently, hooking him up to all kinds of monitors. Now it was about 4:30 in the morning. It had been about ten hours since I first called the ambulance at home. It was not until this point in Birmingham that I became frightened. I looked down at my phone and it was almost dead. I made a quick call to Matt and told him, "Clint is in ICU. No one told us, but I am realizing this is serious. Clint is in trouble."

Matt assured me that he would be in Birmingham as quickly as possible. I sat there in ICU by myself with Clint. No one would really tell me anything except that his doctor would talk to me when he arrived for his rounds later in the morning. I prayed. I was extremely tired, scared, and alone. I was also still sick myself. I left Clint's side to go to the restroom in the lobby. Diarrhea again. I had now been up for over twenty-four hours and had not eaten anything since the soup I had for lunch the day before. I had about 5% battery left on my phone. I sent a text to my boss at the courthouse that I would not be in, told her that I was in Birmingham with my son, that he had been transferred by ambulance. I was trying to do the right thing, but honestly, the courthouse was the least of my worries at that very moment.

Matt arrived at the hospital around 7:30 am. It had only been about five hours since we were together in Huntsville, yet I was so glad to see him walk into the room. Clint was sent for another MRI and an angiogram. Matt and I did a lot of waiting. Finally, later in the afternoon, we met Dr. Fisher.

Dr. Fisher was in his sixties. He stood a little over six feet, had grey hair and the kind of walk that commands a space. He seemed a little arrogant, but not in a bad way, more of in a confident way, as if he knew that he was in a different league from everyone else. As Jessica would later point out, it is not arrogance when you are the real deal. When he came in, he was followed by an entourage of young medical students who were shadowing him and taking notes.

He introduced himself and began, "Clint's brain has really responded to the radiation. In the past three months, since his last MRI, his AVM has shrunk by eighty percent. The problem is that it was supposed to take up to two years for that to happen, a slow process would have been better."

"What does that mean, exactly?"

He continued, "Twenty percent of the AVM still remains, Clint's brain is angry and irritated and is reacting in defense, like someone who has had a major brain injury. This only happens in about three percent of people who receive radiation. But his brain has significant swelling, and we have to stop that."

He went on to explain that they would be putting Clint on high levels of steroids. Steroids are effective to slow brain swelling, at least short term. The goal was to stop or reverse the swelling and hopefully his brain would calm down and adapt to the speed with which the AVM was shrinking.

CHAPTER 19

Later that evening, Clint was moved out of ICU and into a room on the Neurology wing of the hospital. It was a little better for me because there was a couch in his room for me to sleep on and a bathroom in the room. Matt traveled back and forth each day and I stayed with Clint.

They were giving Clint high doses of IV steroids and IV sodium to bring the swelling down. They would not give him much for pain, not anything strong anyway, because a headache was a symptom they did not want to mask. They continued to monitor him, run MRIs, and evaluate his situation. By Wednesday afternoon, Clint's headache was better. He was weak but seemed to be feeling a little better.

Dr. Fisher decided to take him off the IV steroids and start him on oral steroids instead. He said if Clint handled that switch well, he was going to let him go home the next day.

Clint did seem to handle the switch from IV to oral okay. So late Thursday afternoon, Clint was released with strict limitations and restrictions. We were told to continue his medicines and have him rest at home, and to bring him back in two weeks for another MRI. The two-hour drive home from Birmingham wore Clint out and as soon as we got home, he went straight to his bed for a nap.

At 9:00 pm, Clint awoke from his nap complaining of another bad headache and nausea. We called Dr. Fisher's after-hours number and were instructed to bring him right back to UAB. We loaded up the car for the two-hour drive back and Clint was readmitted. It turned out that the oral steroids were not strong enough. Clint's brain had started swelling again. They immediately put him back on the IV regiment.

After two more days in the hospital, there was not much change in the CT scans. The swelling was not coming down enough to even notice, but it also was not continuing to swell. That was good. Clint reported that his head was not hurting any more. Dr. Fisher felt like that was a good sign that the steroids were starting to work.

Dr. Fisher prescribed oral steroids again for Clint, but at a higher dose this time. Clint stayed at the hospital another two days, taking the oral medication there, before they decided to release him to try recuperating at home again. They finally released him after seven days, but again with strict restrictions. He could not go back to work or do anything strenuous, and he could not be left alone. We were told to come back in two weeks for a follow up.

We were also told that Clint could not stay on steroids for a long time. Steroids are a miracle drug for a brain swell. However, when taken for too long, the side effects of the steroids can be worse than what they treat. In fact, in just a week, Clint was already starting to show signs of steroids usage. His face was becoming very swollen. I think they call that moon face. Dr. Fisher also told us that we could not just take Clint off the steroids; he would have to be slowly weaned off them. Dr. Fisher said that we would start doing that after his check up in two weeks.

Once home, I called to speak to my boss at the courthouse. I was told I needed to come in for a face-to-face meeting. Matt took off work to stay with Clint so I could go. My ultimate boss was the Probate Judge. She was genuinely nice and very understanding, and beneath her was my direct supervisor, who was also nice but not nearly as warm toward me as the judge. I went in and honestly felt like a bad child being sent to the principal's office. I saw things from their perspective, I really did. I was new and had missed a lot of work.

I explained to them all that had happened to Clint and where we were in the healing process. I also explained how he could not be left alone for at least the next two weeks. I apologized and told them that I fully understood where my absence had left them, but I would like a little grace and the ability to keep my job and come back as soon as the crisis was over. My supervisor said that the one thing that had upset her the most was that I did not call her initially; I texted instead.

I instantly remembered that morning in the ICU in Birmingham. I was a little shocked that she was upset by that. At the Funky Feather, I always preferred that my employees texted. At that point, I realized that we were both looking at a situation, but from two completely different viewpoints I expressed to her that I truly meant no disrespect by texting; I was honestly struggling and did what I thought was right. Her stance was a little cold towards me at first, but after much deliberation, she and the Judge finally agreed that I could have the two weeks off and return after Clint's follow-up. I hugged them both and thanked them and left. I was grateful, but I also must admit I left feeling a little deflated. I just prayed on the way home for understanding.

Throughout the next week, Clint had no headaches, but he was tired and had a hard time focusing. Our days were spent at home, just resting. By the weekend, I woke up with severe stomach pains. I knew the pain: it was the same pain I had a couple of weeks before, when I was first diagnosed with diverticulitis. I told Matt I was not going to put it off again. He stayed with Clint and I drove myself to the emergency room. I told them that I had diverticulitis again and begged them to please not to readmit me into the hospital.

After four hours there and a CT scan, it was ruled diverticulitis, which I already knew. The ER doctor said it was not as severe as before and that he would prescribe more medicine for me, allowing me to treat at home. What a relief.

I took the medicine for the next ten days and then the pain returned and once again I found myself in the emergency room. This time the doctor told me that since I had three bouts within six weeks, he would be referring me to a surgeon. He said that it was possible that the medicine would not ever adequately be able to treat it and that I may need surgery to remove the infected part of my colon. I was terrified. I went home and read everything about that procedure and realized that it was a major surgery. Something I certainly did not want. The earliest I could get with the surgeon was in October.

In the meantime, the time came for Clint's bi-weekly checkup. He had not had headaches during that period. When Doctor Fisher examined him, there was still swelling but he told us it was time to start slowly weaning him off the steroids. I was instructed to lower his dose by one pill each week for the next four weeks. Dr. Fisher also said that he was not prepared to release Clint to resume regular activities yet. He asked that we keep him at home to rest for at least another two weeks. I asked him if he thought he still needed someone to be with him all day, every day. He looked at me puzzled and I told him that if I needed to stay home with Clint, I was going to lose my job. Dr. Fisher said if we could regularly check on him, it would probably be okay for him to be by himself for short periods.

Matt, Jessica, and I worked out a system. I left for work at 7:30 and took lunch at 11:30. I called Clint and checked in. Matt came home for his lunch at 12:00 to 1:00 and Jessica came home straight after school to check on him until Matt or I could get home from work. It worked, but it made me nervous. Still, I returned to work.

For the next month Clint stayed home and rested. There were no more headaches and vomiting, and he seemed to be handling the adjustment of his medicine well. He took his last dose of steroids on Wednesday evening. Thursday went fine.

On Friday morning the alarm clock sounded at six to wake me up for work. I went into the kitchen to make coffee and realized there was a light on in the living room. I walked in and found Clint sitting on the couch with his head in his hands, tears running from his eyes. I said, "Clint, what's wrong?"

"My head is killing me, Mom. I woke up at 2:00 this morning, and it is just getting worse."

"Why didn't you wake me?"

"I don't know, my head just hurts really, really bad."

"Ah, my poor Clint. Hang on, we are going to get you help."

I told Matt what was going on. He came into the living room and sat with Clint, while I went to the bedroom to get dressed. I called the local hospital and asked them if we got Clint there, could they call for transport to Birmingham. I knew that the way Clint's head was hurting, his brain was swelling again, I also knew time was of the essence.

They told me that I would have to come through their ER and allow them to run test and evaluate him before they could call med flight or an ambulance to take him somewhere else. Matt and I discussed it and knew that would waste time. We decided to take a chance and drive him straight to Birmingham ourselves. I told Matt that if we had trouble along the way, we could always call 911 in the town we were closest to, but we both knew he needed to be in Birmingham as soon as possible.

It seemed to take forever to get to Birmingham because of rush hour traffic. All the while, Clint's head was pounding, and he was nauseous.

CHAPTER 20

We went through the Emergency Room in Birmingham. But since Clint had been there the month before, they were aware of Clint's medical condition. When we told them what was going on, they took him straight back into a room. He was seen by the resident neurologist on call, Dr. Laskay. We had met Dr. Laskay before, when we were there earlier. He was probably in his late thirties or early forties. As a resident doctor, he was working on call about fourteen-hour shifts at a time. I remembered from our stay before that it seemed anytime Clint needed a doctor after-hours, it was always Dr. Laskay that would come. He seemed very capable and smart, but he also seemed very hurried and a little put out. Honestly, I was not impressed with his bedside manner, but I was glad to see a doctor who was familiar with Clint and our situation. As soon as he came into the room, he ordered a CT scan. Then we waited.

Clint's speech was a little slurred and he kept telling me that his head was really hurting. Dr. Laskay came back into our room about an hour later and told us that Clint's brain was swelling again. Cranial Edema he called it. He said that he was going to admit him back into the hospital. He told us that Dr. Fisher was on vacation however, he had already spoken to him by phone. Their plan was to start Clint back on steroids to get him stable and then when Dr. Fisher got back on Monday, he planned to do surgery.

I had so many questions and concerns, but Doctor Laskay would not give me any other information. He said it was not in his expertise. He stated that we would need to wait until Monday when Dr. Fisher returned to ask our questions, and that he did not want to give us wrong information. I later realized that he probably knew more, but as a resident doctor, he had to stay in his lane; he really was not allowed to tell us anything. I was upset though. How could he spring the news on us that Clint would be having brain surgery on Monday, yet not be able to answer a single question.

I made a quick call to the courthouse. I spoke directly to the Judge and explained what was going on. I told her that, regretfully, I felt it was best if I just resigned. I did not know what was going to happen, but I knew that we would be in Birmingham for a while. She was understanding.

I contacted Travis and told him that we were at the hospital again. I told him that they were talking about doing surgery on Clint on Monday but would not tell me anything more until his neurosurgeon was back. He seemed concerned but just told me to keep him posted.

I also contacted my brother, Jimmy, and some of my cousins; we had a group text going. They were a refuge and lifeline for me and Matt. They instantly started praying.

We were told that we would have to stay in the ER until a room on the Neurology floor became available. They started Clint on the steroids and gave him something to ease the nausea. He finally dozed off. I was relieved that he was getting relief. I knew he was exhausted.

At about two in the afternoon, when Clint awoke from his nap, he was confused and unable to speak properly. He also could not raise his left hand and his face was visibly swollen. I ran out of the room and summoned a nurse. She called Dr. Laskay and then a bunch of nurses came in and swept Clint hurriedly out of the room for another emergency CT scan. We waited and waited again. Clint's speech gradually got better, and he was not as confused, but he still had a headache. It just seemed to be taking a long time to get any answers.

At 4:45pm, there was a knock on the door. A lady in her fifties came in and introduced herself as an anesthesiologist. She said she was there to ask us questions about Clint to get him ready for his surgery scheduled for 7:30 am the next morning.

"Surgery in the morning? What surgery?" I asked.

"Oh, have they not come to talk to you yet? The doctor ordered it for in the morning. We have the operating room reserved already."

I said, "No, no one has come to talk to me. I haven't even heard the results of his last CT scan. Dr. Fisher is out of town. Which doctor ordered this?"

She apologized and said that she had come into the room before the surgeon or Dr. Laskay had had the chance to talk to me. She said they would be coming in to talk to us soon. We answered the questions that she had, and she left.

Matt, Clint, and I had no idea what was going on. I was very confused, but also very scared. I said to Matt, "They must have found something really bad to move the surgery up before Dr. Fisher gets back from vacation. I am going to try and find someone to tell us what was going on."

I went to the nurse's station in the ER and asked the nurse, who had been tending to Clint all day, what was going on. She could tell that I was upset. She told me that she would talk to the ER doctor and they would be right in. It did not take long before she and the ER doctor came into our room and told us that they did not know anything about Clint being scheduled for surgery. They told us that they just paged Dr. Laskay, but as far as they knew, the CT scan results were not back yet. They were as confused as we were.

It took Dr. Laskay another forty-five minutes to come into our room. He seemed annoyed, although I could not tell if his annoyance was directed towards us. He looked at us and bluntly stated, "I don't know why the anesthesiologist was in here, but she was wrong. There is no surgery scheduled for tomorrow. I already told you that it will be on Monday, when Dr. Fisher comes back."

"She was specific and had all of Clint's information. How did she get that if there isn't surgery? Also, what did the CT Scan show?"

Dr. Laskay stated, "Dr. Fisher is the only one who can make that call, and he would direct me and no one else. Again, I do not know why she was in here, but there is no surgery scheduled for tomorrow!" he then continued, "I haven't had time to get back down here yet, but the scan results showed no change. I believe that his sudden decline earlier was caused by a seizure. I have ordered a twenty-four-hour EEG to monitor it, and I plan to increase his anti-seizure meds." He then kind of dismissed any further discussion and left the room.

A few minutes later, the nurse came in and said they had a room for Clint. That was great news. We had been in the Emergency Room for over ten hours. We settled in. Matt left to go back to Arab and be with Jessica. I slept on the couch/bench next to Clint.

By Saturday morning, the nurses had finally given Clint something for the pain. He had also been getting steroids for about twenty-four hours. With the combination of the two, he was feeling better but was still very

103

confused.

When Matt came in the next morning, Clint started telling him every detail correctly about getting up at two in the morning with a headache and coming to the hospital. He struggled as he pronounced the word "hospital". He told Matt that he came to the hospital "Today." Matt told him that he knew about the headache and trip to the hospital because he had been with him when it happened. Then he reminded Clint that all of that had happened the day before. Clint was insistent that it was not the day before; it was today. Matt and I both told Clint again that it had been the day before and with that Clint became very argumentative and agitated. We knew he was simply confused and frustrated.

As the day went on, Clint still had a headache. He stated that it was not nearly as severe as the headache he had the day before. In fact, he cracked a few jokes. But he still struggled with saying simple words. However, he did remember that Dr. Laskay told us that the brain swell was called a Cranial Edema. Clint randomly told me and Matt that Bruce Lee had died from Cranial Edema. He remembered that fact and said it perfectly. It's odd how the brain works.

Dr. Laskay made his rounds. He was efficient, but his bedside manner was still not much better. He was hurried and would still not tell us anything more than that we would have to wait on Dr. Fisher.

I tried to press him for some information such as what to expect with the surgery, recovery, prognosis… He would not comment on any of that, but he looked at me and said, "All I can tell you right now is prayer is powerful, just pray."

As he turned to walk out, Clint said, "Hey, Dr. Laskay."

"Yes."

"I just want to tell you; you are one of my favorite doctors ever!"

Clint was sincere. He meant what he said, but I could tell it caught Dr. Laskay off guard and kind of disarmed him a bit. He paused for a second, let out a small grin, and then responded, "Thanks, buddy."

Sunday was a day spent in great deliberation and prayer. I had done some reading up on brain surgery. It was really hitting me hard how serious this was. And as Clint's legal guardian, it would be up to me to make the decision for Clint on how to proceed. But in everything I read and by the fact that Dr. Laskay would not discuss anything with me, just kept referring me to Dr. Fisher, I realized how bad this could go. Clint could be left with permanent brain damage or more severe disabilities. However, without the surgery, he could die.

Clint overheard me telling Matt that I was worried and did not want him to have to go through surgery. Clint said, "Mom, I want to have surgery."

"You want to have surgery?"

"Yes, my head really hurts… bad. If I have surgery, I will feel better and it won't hurt anymore."

"Clint, do you realize that the surgery will take a while to recover from? You know it won't be easy, right?"

He said, "I know, but that's okay. I don't want to have a headache anymore."

Wow, that was quite a revelation. My poor baby and the pain he must be in. At the same time, I wished that Clint could participate in the decision making based on the complete understanding of the risk as well as the result. I knew he did not understand the full impact of what was about to happen. I felt the weight on my shoulders.

Sunday night was long and nerve-wracking. Matt stayed with us and slept in the recliner in the room and I slept on the couch/bench again, although I can tell you that neither of us really slept much at all. We were both apprehensive. The nurses were in and out all night and Clint was restless.

At about 6am on Monday, the hospital door opened and in walked my cousin Suzanne and her husband Dewayne. I was so glad to see them there. They had traveled down the night before and gotten a hotel to be at the hospital with us this morning.

At about seven, Dr. Fisher came in. Finally! I had a list of questions written down. I asked Matt and Suzanne to jump in too if I missed something. I asked every question that I could think of. Dr. Fisher was very attentive and answered them all. He told me that the bottom line was that the brain cannot continue to swell, and Clint cannot stay on steroids long term. He stated that they had exhausted every option they had to help him, short of the surgery.

I said to him, "When Dr. Stetler recommended the radiation last year, he said this surgery was too dangerous."

"And that was true. A year ago, radiation was the best choice. I would have made the same recommendation," he continued to explain, "but since that time, the situation has changed. I feel that we can successfully remove the rest of the AVM and the prognosis will be good. But the surgery is really not optional anymore. Unfortunately, Clint is one of the rare three percent of people whose body overreacted to the radiation, so at this point, we really have no other choice."

"Dr. Fisher, I have one last question…and it is the most important one to me."

"Okay, what is it?"

"You are aware that I have to make this decision, you know that Clint isn't capable of understanding everything fully, right?"

He said, "Yes."

"Well…then this is my question: If you were in my exact situation and this was your son, and knowing what you know, and knowing you would be the one to have to make the decision to go forward with this surgery, would you make the decision for this surgery if this were your son."

Without hesitation, he responded, "I absolutely would."

He looked at me very sincerely and stated again, "This is serious. There is no doubt, life or death serious, but there really are no other options. If this were my son, I would authorize the surgery."

I said, "Okay, then. I will, too."

CHAPTER 21

Within the hour, they came to get Clint to take him for surgery prep. We were all allowed to go and stay with him. He was being so brave. I on the other hand was a nervous wreck. I was not prepared mentally. There was a flurry of activity, with doctors and nurses and anesthesiologist all coming in and out to get him ready. I remember looking down at Clint and thinking how innocent and vulnerable he was. I started crying. He said, "Mom, please don't cry. I going to be glad not have headaches anymore."

At 9am, they took him away to begin the surgery. We were directed to the operating waiting room. I was given a pager and told that periodically during the procedure I would be paged to come to the front desk for information. Matt, Suzanne, Dewayne, and I settled into a corner of the waiting room.

We tried to make small talk and keep our spirits uplifted, but the wait was agonizing. After we had been there for about an hour and a half, I was paged for the first time. I went to the desk and the receptionist told me that there was a nurse on the phone waiting to speak with me. My heart sank as I prepared myself. I picked up the phone and said, "Hello."

"I was just calling to let you know that that he is asleep now with the anesthesia and the surgery has begun. He is doing well so far. We will call you back in a couple of hours to let you know how things are going."

"Okay, thank you."

We decided to go and eat some breakfast and just try to do something other than sitting in the waiting room for a few minutes. I carried the pager with me. Once we were in the cafeteria, I picked up my phone and texted Travis to let him know that Clint was in surgery. His response was a little unnerving. He texted back: "Surgery?"

"Yes, you know we have been at the hospital since Friday morning, and I told you then that Clint would probably be having surgery on Monday."

107

He continued, "Yeah, but I thought you would let me know if they were going to do that."

I just remember feeling frustrated. How could he expect me stay in touch with him, with everything going on, yet, he had not reached out to us at all since Friday or come to the hospital. I just let it go.

We finished eating and went back up to the waiting room. We were there for another two hours before I got the second page. The nurse on the other end of the phone told me that they were about halfway through and Clint was doing fine so far. Then we waited some more.

Jessica found a friend who was willing to ride with her to Birmingham. She called me and asked if she could drive down, she could not stand it, not being there with us. I knew how important it was for her to be there; she missed us, and she was worried about her brother, but I was scared for her to drive to and navigate Birmingham by herself for the first time. I hesitated but she reassured me that she could do it. Matt and Dewayne both said if she got into trouble or got lost, they would leave the hospital to go and help her. I told her she could come.

She made the drive to Birmingham without any trouble. But once she got into downtown, she did get lost trying to find the hospital. She kept calling Matt and he was trying to determine where she was and how to get her back to where we were. That was stressful for me. I was worried about her. Finally, about 3:00 o'clock she told Matt she was at the parking garage and would be up shortly. I had never been so happy as I was to see Jessica come off the elevator.

By about 4 o'clock, Clint had been in surgery for almost six hours. We were expecting Doctor Fisher to come out and talk to us when the surgery was over. Instead, the last page I received was from a nurse letting me know that Clint was out of surgery and heading back to the ICU unit. I was told to go there right away.

When we got up to the ICU floor, we were met by another nurse who told us that normally the family was not allowed to see a patient this soon after surgery. She told me that patients usually went for recovery first, however, in Clint's case, as soon as he came out of surgery, he was crying out for his mom. She told us that he was very agitated, and they felt that if I was with him, it may help calm him down. She warned me that because the surgery was still so fresh, she did not want me to be frightened when I saw him. She told me that he was still under anesthesia, and they had not had the time to change all the bedding yet. After our conversation, I thought that I was prepared to see him, but I really was not.

I had not spoken to Doctor Fisher or to anyone else on the operating team, so I really did not know how he had done; all I knew was that he wanted to see me. As Matt and I were led into his room, I was shocked by what I saw. Clint had all kinds of drainage tubes and other tubes coming directly from inside of his head. There was blood all over his pillow. He was uncontrollably crying, combative, and agitated. I immediately went over to his bed and tried to reassure him that I was there, and to calm him down. He looked right through me. It was as if he neither knew who I was nor that I was even there. The nurse at his bedside was trying to get him settled in. She assured me that Clint's behavior was normal at this stage after surgery because he was still not awake. I just remember being stunned by what I was seeing. My poor Clint. I just wanted to make this better. I just wanted to understand. I looked at the nurse and asked how the surgery went. He told me that he did not know that I would have to wait until Doctor Fisher came to talk to me. I remember thinking that should have happened first. I should have known what was going on and been better prepared, before being led into ICU.

After a few minutes we had to walk out. We went into the waiting room and was met by Suzanne, Dewayne, Jessica, and her friend, all anxiously wanting to know how he was. I believe they could tell that we were upset. They began to ask me what was going on and all I could say was: "It is not good. I don't think he recognized me. He is crying and screaming, and there is blood everywhere."

Jessica asked if she could go back to see him. I told her that I was not sure it was a good idea, that he was still trying to wake up and they had not cleaned him up yet. She said, "Mom, please let me go back."

She walked back to see him and then reemerged into the waiting room moments later, as white as a sheet. She said, "Mom you were right. I was not expecting that."

I wanted to speak to Dr. Fisher. I was told that he would be talking to me later, but that he was currently in another surgery. At that point, no one was really telling me anything. We spent the next few hours with Clint. The nurses in ICU were at his bedside continually. They never left. They were monitoring the drainage tubes, Clint's vitals, and charting every detail. Clint looked scared and confused. His arms and hands were contorted at his chest and he was crying a lot.

At about 7pm, Dr. Fisher, Dr. Laskay, and their entourage came into Clint's ICU bay. Dr. Fisher was not aware that I had been told to go to ICU. He stated that he came into the operating waiting room to talk to us after surgery, but we were not there, and he had another scheduled surgery behind Clint's. That is why it took hours for us to get information.

Dr. Fisher said that the surgery had gone well and now Clint just needed time to heal. I asked him why Clint was acting like he was, and he said it was a combination of the brain swelling from the AVM and from the surgery and the effects of the anesthesia. He assured me that by the next day, we should see some improvement, and told me not worry. He said that Clint just needed rest and time to heal.

We walked back out to the waiting room to tell the family what Dr. Fisher said. It was time for Jessica and her friend to leave to head back to Arab too. After we finished talking, Dewayne reached out and handed Matt a card. Matt said, "What is this?"

"It is a room key to the hotel adjacent to the hospital. While you were back there with Clint, Suzanne and I walked over there and paid for a room for you guys to have a place to sleep tonight."

We were shocked. I said, "Really? I appreciate that, but you shouldn't have. I can only imagine how expensive this was, and I really don't think I should leave Clint."

Dewayne said, "They will not let you stay in the ICU with Clint after a certain hour and that only leaves this waiting room for you to sleep. You can't do that." He continued, "The hotel is in the parking lot. You really should get rest tonight. If he needs you, the hospital staff can call you, and you will literally just be right downstairs."

Around eight pm, Jessica and her friend left, and Suzanne and Dewayne did as well. Matt and I stayed, going back and forth between Clint's bedside and the ICU waiting room. Finally, around midnight, Matt insisted that we leave and take advantage of the room Suzanne and Dewayne had graciously paid for us. I left my phone number with the nurse, and we took the elevator to the bottom floor of the hospital.

It was a really nice hotel, and I must admit that getting a hot shower and a real bed was rejuvenating. I did not realize how exhausted I was until my head hit the pillow. Sleeping on a hospital bench/couch for three nights along with all the long waits is really not good for the soul.

We set the alarm clock for 6am, downed a cup of coffee and headed straight back to ICU. I was expecting to see a world of change in Clint, but to my dismay, there was really no change at all. When we came into his room, he instantly started crying again. His left hand and arm were curled up at his torso. He in fact had no use of it. His left leg was weak also. He had tubes of all sorts coming from the surgery site, as well as IV's and monitors. I walked to his bedside. He clearly recognized me but could not speak. Tears just ran down his face.

When Dr. Fisher came in, and while he did not seem overly alarmed, I could tell that he was not expecting to see Clint in that shape either. He ordered another CT scan and when the results came back, he told us that Clint still had significant swelling in his brain, and it what was causing the severe neurological difficulties he was having. Dr. Fisher felt that was normal, one day after surgery. He thought that the swelling would come down, and things would improve over time, but he wasn't hundred percent sure. He acknowledged that he was expecting Clint to be better than this, but each surgery is different, and the brain is complicated. He reassured us that he would be surprised if things did not improve in time. He just kept telling us not to worry, that with each day, things would get better.

Later in the afternoon, they sedated Clint again to put in a central PIC line, right into the artery in his neck area. They did this to be able to administer medicine quicker, and to keep the IV's from bothering Clint.

Clint's head had been shaved and a bandage covered his head. While they had cleaned him up several times, blood still seeped through. He had drainage tubes coming from his head through the bandages to keep the fluid from building up, and his brain from the swelling. The tubes were gravity fed, as a result, Clint's height in the bed had to be leveled against the level of the tube coming out of his head. If Clint slid down in the bed or if we adjusted his bed at all, an ICU nurse would have to come in to make sure the tube was leveled to ensure that all his brain fluid did not gush right out of his head. Necessary and lifesaving, but horrifying, nonetheless.

Clint was only able to say three words. He said, "Yes, please." or "Almost" robotically. If you asked him if he were thirsty, he would respond with, "Yes, please." Or if he was in pain, "Yes, please." When he was trying to communicate with us, he would point at something and say, "Almost." If we could not figure out what he was trying to communicate, he would become agitated and start yelling, "Almost…almost…almost…" while pointing frantically with his right hand. He was also under the influence of pain medications, so he would slip in and out of sleep. When he was awake, he spent much of the time yelling or crying uncontrollably. Matt and I were with him all day, but it was hard to watch. When we needed a break, we would just step out into the waiting room and then right back in.

Jessica came back to Birmingham in the afternoon. She stayed in the waiting room and when we went out, we would give her updates. I told her that she could go back, but she decided not to go back to see him. She told me that she was not prepared to see Clint like that again. She sat patiently in the waiting room for most of the day by herself. I told her she should go home and let us call her if something changed. She refused to leave.

When Dr. Fisher came in for his evening rounds, he confirmed again that Clint's condition was caused by the severe brain swelling from both the AVM and the surgery. He told us that while the side effects were not what he was expecting or what they had hoped for, and that he could not guarantee improvement, he did feel that it would improve with time. He told us that he wanted to give it a couple of days before he would allow himself to be worried about any prognosis and we should do the same. I was very confused: like what did he mean, that was not what he expected, and he could not guarantee improvement?

The day was sad and exhausting, physically and mentally draining. Around 10 pm, Matt and I decided to go back to the hotel for the night, we quickly realized that we could not do that every night. As I had expected, it was so expensive, everything at the hospital was expensive from food, to parking to lodging. But for that night, I was once again thankful for a bed and a shower. Jessica stayed with us. The next morning, we headed back to the ICU first thing.

Clint was still not much better, still agitated, still only saying his two phrases, and looking at me as if he didn't know me or was trying to place me. The nurses from ICU were in and out of the room all day. Others would come in for different evaluations.

The doctors did their rounds. Dr. Fisher tried to present an optimistic front to me, but I could tell that he was a little concerned that Clint was not responding as he expected. Dr. Fisher put Clint on a diuretic to try to remove the fluid off his brain, keeping the drain in, upping his steroid, and adding a salt medicine too. They were trying to do all they could think to do to get the brain swelling down.

He also ordered an EEG; he wanted to know if possibly seizures could be causing him to be in the semi catatonic state that he was in. He also instructed that Clint should have no visitors after 8 o'clock, and the lights and curtains were to be drawn in his ICU room. He ordered less checking of his vitals by the nurses during the evening. He said, perhaps some of the confusion could be attributed to sleep deprivation in addition to everything else. I was told that the no disturbance order also included me. He told me that I needed to go home. I told him that I would not.

Dr Fisher said, "Clint needs uninterrupted sleep. He will be in ICU for a while and you cannot stay up for days on end, and you cannot sleep in the chairs in the waiting room. You have been at the hospital for the past six days. You need to take care of you in order to take care of him." He continued, "Please, go home."

When he walked out of the room, I told Matt that I was not leaving Clint, but Matt sided with the doctor. We stayed until about six or seven and then left for home. We did not make it out of the parking lot of the hospital before I was crying like a baby, I felt like I was letting Clint down by leaving. Matt assured me that he would be okay.

After getting settled in at home, I realized that I was not in a good place mentally. Clint was not Clint. Although the doctor kept telling me to give it time, I felt discouraged and felt that I may have made the wrong decision agreeing for them to do the surgery. As soon as that thought hit me, I reminded myself that I had no other choice—without the surgery he could have died. I felt guilty being home, but also realized being at the hospital was causing me some insanity. I showered and snuggled with my dogs, ate supper, and called the nurse before we went to bed to check on Clint. They told me his vitals were good and he was resting fine.

The next morning, I was up by 5am and heading back to Birmingham. Matt had to go back to work so he couldn't go with me. When I went in, Clint seemed to recognize me, but he was still not much better. He was swollen everywhere; he was not able to use his left arm at all and was still not able to speak. I tried to put up a brave façade, but it was not easy. I just kept praying that God would make this be okay.

Even though I had left Arab so early, I had still missed the morning rounds with the doctor. I asked the nurse what they had charted. She said she thought that everything was the same, no change, but she could not really tell me for sure. She told me that she would page the doctor on call, Dr. Laskay. And she did.

Hours went by and Dr. Laskay had still not come into the room. The nurse paged him again. About half an hour later he came in, followed by the nurse. I could tell that he was not happy about being paged. I looked at him and said, "I just wanted to know what Dr. Fisher said this morning when he saw Clint. I am concerned that there hasn't been much change since surgery."

He retorted, "It will take time, and I am sorry that I didn't come when paged, but I have a lot of patients, and I don't have time to come and talk to every family member at the drop of a hat."

"Wait, What?"

When I processed what he said, It pissed me off instantly and without thinking about it first, I responded, "Uh, no disrespect, but I don't give a damn about how many other patients you have. I care about this patient, Clint. I will continue to advocate for him! If you are too busy to be bothered with his family, with me, then I don't know what to say to you."

He and I just stared at each other for a couple of seconds. It felt like an eternity. Dr. Laskay broke the silence and said coldly, "I am here now, what are your questions?"

He answered all my questions and concerns, but the air was thick with tension. After he left, the nurse made eye contact with me. I said to her, "I am sorry. I probably should not have said that to the doctor. I know that he is busy, but what he said really upset me."

She said, "Honey, don't you apologize to me at all. I would have been upset, too. It was uncalled for. You are Clint's mother. if my child were in here, I would be the same way."

"Thank you for that."

That was the end of it as far as I was concerned. About an hour later, a hospital administrator came into the room and asked if he could speak to me. I could tell he was someone official because he was wearing a business suit, not scrubs.

I said, "Sure, what's up?"

"I want to personally apologize for the way Dr. Laskay treated you earlier, that is against everything we stand for at UAB. I was wondering if you would be willing to tell me your side of what happened."

"I can, but as far as I am concerned, I said my piece directly to Dr. Laskay and it is over and done with. How do you even know about it, anyway? I did not complain to anyone?"

He said, "The nurse that was in the room reported him. She is obligated to do so whenever there is any kind of conflict in a room, especially when she thinks someone from the hospital is in the wrong. We do not want any patient or family not to be treated with courtesy and respect at all times."

"I get and appreciate that, but I don't want him to be in any trouble. I know he has a lot on the go. It was not that big of a deal. It's over now, all is good."

He continued, "Thanks for that. But he is a resident doctor. He represents us and that is not an acceptable way to treat our patient's family. So again, on behalf of UAB, we are sorry that he wasn't more professional and respectful."

With that he left. While Dr. Laskay was a little arrogant, he did not really bother me. He and I had worked it out amongst ourselves. I did not want the nurse to report him. I did not want it to go further. I did not want him to be in trouble. Besides, Clint had already decided that Dr. Laskay was his favorite doctor ever, right?

I do not know what happened after that. I never heard anything further.

But from that point on, every time Dr. Laskay made rounds with Dr. Fisher or on his own, or every time I had any questions for him, he was super nice. Poor guy, I really did feel bad for him and the about the whole situation.

Later in that afternoon, I received a text from Travis. His text read something to the effect that he was thinking about coming to visit Clint today, if I thought he was up to receiving a visitor. It was the first I had heard from Travis since the Monday, four days before, when I told him that Clint was in surgery.

I wrote back: "Travis, you can come, but I am not sure if Clint will be up to entertaining a visitor. You do realize that he is in ICU?"

I was furious.

He replied, "Would another day be better?"

What part of this was he not understanding? I texted: "Travis, Clint is in ICU. He is not doing well. I have been here night and day for the past week. I cannot tell you when he may be better. I wish that I could. But better or not, you are his dad. You can come be here whenever you want!"

He texted back, "I didn't know. I will come this afternoon."

Later that afternoon, Travis texted again to let me know that he was at the hospital. I told him how to get to the ICU waiting room and told him I would meet him. When he got off the elevator, I tried to explain Clint's condition to him and prepare him. I told him where Clint's room was, and he went back. I used the opportunity to go down to the lobby and buy a coffee. I came back up and sat in the waiting room.

Travis was back with Clint for about an hour. When he reemerged into the waiting room he was visibly shaken, and I could tell he had been crying. He just looked at me and kind of mouthed, "I had no idea." For a split second, I felt bad for him, honestly. Sympathetic. He sat in the waiting room with me and talked for probably another hour. He told me he planned to come back the next day and with that he left.

The rest of my day was spent in Clint's room. The doctors made their rounds, but really could not give any new information. I texted Matt off and on during the day, but mostly I felt scared, alone, and overwhelmingly sad. I finally left the hospital around 8pm. I had been there for over twelve hours and I just could not do it anymore. I took the long walk from Clint's room to the elevator, went down the long corridor towards the parking garage. UAB is huge, so it literally took about ten minutes of hard walking to get from Clint's room to the parking garage. When I finally reached the lobby to the garage, I reached into my pocket for my parking ticket. It was not there. I started frantically searching everywhere. I did not have it.

It cost eight dollars a day to park, but if you did not have your ticket, the charge was like thirty dollars. Normally, that would be just a minor setback.

I walked over to the attendants. There was a lady and a younger gentleman behind the counter. The lady looked at me and said cheerfully, "Hi, how can we help you?"

"Um, I…"

That was all that I got out before I started just bawling. A grown woman, standing there sobbing uncontrollably.

She said, "Oh my, what is wrong?" There was a brief pause and she realized, "Did you lose your parking ticket?"

I nodded.

She said, "Don't cry over that, honey, we can get you another one, we can fix it."

Through sniffles, I replied, "Yes, but I can't afford to pay thirty dollars a day to park my car. I have already been here every day for a week, I just can't pay that."

The young man next to her jumped in, "You do not have to, we got you, there is no need to cry. I am going to fix this for you. How about eight dollars, how does that sound?"

I nodded again. I could not stop crying. I felt like a fool. The attendants did help me get another ticket. I paid the money and headed to my car.

I texted Matt and told him that I was on my way home. And then I sat in the car for a few minutes and cried more, harder than I had cried in a long time. I was trying to pull it together for the two-hour drive home. Then it hit me, the date- it was October 11, the seventh anniversary of Max's death. It had not occurred to me, not consciously anyway. Then I felt guilty for not remembering before then. With Clint's condition, the anniversary of

Max's death, being at the hospital alone, the incidence with the doctor, and with Travis, the lost parking ticket, it was just all I could take for the day. It was not a good day. I made it home, ate dinner, called the hospital, showered, and went straight to bed.

The next day was a Saturday, Matt had to stay and tend to the Funky Feather, but Jessica was able to come back to the hospital with me. She told me that she felt she could go back and see Clint. She had prepared herself.

When we got there, Clint did seem to have more recognition of us and seemed relieved that we were there. There seemed to be some minor improvement. I was encouraged by the difference. He was speaking a little, still confusing words and saying the wrong words, but he was talking. Progress. Jessica and I went back and forth all day between his room and the waiting room. I was grateful that she was with me. It was good for me to have some company. I was also mindful of the fact that being in ICU was difficult for her.

While she and I were in his room, the occupational therapist came in to evaluate whether Clint could swallow. Apparently when I went home the night before a nurse had given Clint something to drink and he choked a little. The nurse had requested this evaluation. The therapist had all kinds of foods and drinks and she put dye in them. She then tried to insert a camera through Clint's nose to observe his swallowing. I was standing beside him and Jessica was at the foot of the bed. Clint did not understand what was happening, he was afraid, I could see it in his eyes. He became very agitated when they tried to insert the camera and started flailing and moaning. He fought to pull the camera out and it caused his nose to bleed. He could not talk. Instead he started crying. The staff tried to restrain his hands and do the test again. It was hard to watch, I had to walk away. Jessica looked at me, smiled sweetly and said, "Mom, I've got this."

I went to the other side of the room and stared out the window. I could hear everything, but I just was not able to watch. Jessica moved into my spot on the side of the bed and held Clint's hand. She kept telling him that she was there, and that he was doing good. She said, "Clint, I am proud of you for being so brave."

I wish she could have known how proud I was of her at that moment as well. So much maturity and compassion for her brother and for me.

They were finally able to complete the test, and determined that Clint was having trouble swallowing thin things such as drinks, but did better with thicker things like Jell-O. They stated that they were going to recommend that Clint start getting food again, something he had not had in six days, but anything given to him would require a thickening agent be added to help him swallow it. They told me that swallowing is a function of the brain, and because his brain is swollen, it is just not communicating quickly enough with his throat to swallow thin things before they go down the wrong pipe. They said it would improve. I felt very frustrated that he was put through that. And I also could not wrap my brain around him being able to eat meals in the condition that he was in.

In no time I saw for myself how he ate when they brought in a tray. I cut up everything for him, like I used to when he was a toddler. Using his right hand, he was able to feed himself. Much of it wound up in his lap, but overall, he did good.

As the day progressed, he looked at me and said very slowly, "Mom, I home," and then tears started running down his face.

I said, "You want to go home?"

"Yes."

"I know, baby. That's why you have to keep working to get better, so we can get you home."

He said again, "Home," and loosely pointed at the door of ICU.

"I know baby, I know. You will, soon, I promise."

It was so sad to see, however, I was also elated. He spoke and he communicated an actual thought.

Later in the afternoon, my friend, Susan, came to the hospital. She brought Clint a little stuffed dinosaur. It sat in his bed with him from that point on. Susan being there was great for Jessica and me, too. She is one of those people who just always seem to say and do the right thing. She lifted our spirits.

Shortly after she left, Travis came back with his wife, Juanita, her daughter, son in law, and grandchild. While they spent time with Clint, Jessica and I walked down to the coffee shop and gave them some time together. After

Travis finished with his visit, he asked me to please allow him to help more. He said he would do anything to help. I was grateful, honestly.

I said, "Travis, if you are serious, I do have a doctor's appointment with the surgeon back home on Thursday. I have had the appointment booked for almost a month. They think I may have to have surgery because of diverticulitis. Is there any way that you could come here on Thursday to be with Clint?" If you cannot, Matt is planning to take the day off, but he has already missed a lot of work, if you could come here, that would be a huge help."

Without hesitation, he responded, "Absolutely, I can do it and I would be honored to do it. I hate seeing Clint like this. I will do whatever I can to help."

I thought that went well.

After they left, we went back into Clint's room. He was able to use a bed pan, first time since before surgery. The nurse said it was a good sign, a sign that things are starting to work again. He also became aware that he had a catheter, and that it was bugging him. That was not a good thing for him. I am sure it was extremely uncomfortable. I was glad, not at his discomfort, but just at the fact he was expressing discomfort. As Jessica and I left that night, I felt hopeful. It was small steps, but Clint recognized us, spoke a few words, ate, expressed discomfort, and he wanted to go home. I felt those were all steps in the right direction.

CHAPTER 22

On Sunday, Matt was able to go back to Birmingham with me. When we arrived, we found out that the doctor had ordered another CT scan during the night. They wanted to see the status of the swelling. They had taken Clint for the scan at three in the morning. It was not a test of urgency, just scheduling. As we found out in the many days and weeks we were at the hospital, they do not schedule their work at convenient times for the patient. That was fine, but poor Clint was tired, as a result, he did not seem to be doing quite as well as he had been the day before.

The CT scan showed that there had not been any change. The swelling had not gone down, but it also had not gotten worse either. Dr. Fisher also scheduled another angiogram, to take place on Monday. He wanted to confirm that they had in fact gotten all the AVM and that the swelling was not being caused by something vascular. If that was the case, that would have to be addressed, but if not, he still believed it was a waiting game. He felt the swelling would eventually subside.

Matt's son, Michael, and my cousin, Suzanne, both called and told us they were coming to Birmingham to see Clint.

Suzanne and Dewayne arrived first. We sat in the waiting room and talked for a bit and then Michael and Desiree arrived. I walked back with Suzanne to ICU to see Clint. He recognized her but could not pronounce her name. He was really struggling with his words and was not doing as well as he had the day before. I told Suzanne that I believed it was because he had not slept much the night before.

Matt brought Michael and Desiree back to see him as well, then we decided to go out and get something to eat and give Clint a chance to rest without disruption. It also gave us a distraction for an hour or so.

After we ate, we went back to ICU and I went to check on Clint. He was sleeping. We all sat in the ICU waiting room and talked a little longer and then Michael, Desiree, Suzanne, and Dewayne left to go home.

Matt and I went in with Clint. Clint was still struggling to find the right words, but he was communicating, and what he was communicating at that time was that the catheter was really hurting him. It had been inserted for a week and was causing him stress and discomfort. I first spoke to one nurse, who said there really was not much that could be done. Later when I brought it up to another nurse, she said that she would talk to the doctor to see if Clint could have a condom catheter. The doctor agreed to it. I had never heard of such, but basically a condom catheter slips over the private part area, and has a tube attached to the end of it. With it on, when Clint needed to pee, he just peed into the condom, and it funneled the urine through the tube into the bag. Well, that was a game changer!

Eventually anyway. But initially, because Clint had the catheter all week, and because using the bathroom while lying in the bed seems unnatural to us all, Clint was really having a hard time peeing. The nurse kept coming in to see if he had gone. At first it was okay that he had not, but as the day went on the nurse started threatening Clint that if he did not go soon, they were going to have to reinsert the Catheter. Clint adamantly did not want that, but the threat of that and the pressure of having to go, was really stressing him out. Matt kept telling him it was okay just relax and go. I kept turning on the sink and running water, we were doing everything we could to help him.

The nurse came back in and said that she was going to give him about another half an hour and if he still had not gone, the catheter was going back in. That threat created real pressure. About ten minutes later, he finally went! He started laughing and giving a thumbs up. Matt and I were giving him high fives and clapping. Between the three of us, there was true happiness, someone walking by ICU, would have thought that we just won the lottery or something, but it was a milestone, and seeing Clint laugh over the situation was icing on the cake that day.

Monday, October 14, one week since surgery, I went back to Birmingham by myself. Matt had to go to work and Jessica was back in school. They came and got Clint around eight in the morning for his angiogram, a procedure where they run a camera up to the brain through an artery in the groin area. After the test, Clint had to lie still until the insertion site clotted, so as not to bleed out. It is a relatively common and safe procedure, in fact, he had several of them since this all began, but it was still nerve racking for me.

After he got back to the room, I realized this was going to be a good day. Clint's language was still not right, at all, but he was starting to pick up more words. He was also communicating nonverbally better too. He seemed in good spirits. He was also getting better with feeding himself. He still had no use of his left arm, and his dexterity in his right arm was a little shaky, but he was doing better with it.

At lunch time, I told Clint that I was going to walk down to the hospital cafeteria. I was gone for about thirty minutes and when I got back to Clint's room, he said, "Mom, AVM gone."

"What?"

"Doctor came, AVM gone"

I could not believe what I was hearing, not only the news that they had gotten all the AVM—Hallelujah—but also that it was Clint who just relayed that information to me. I walked out to the nurse's station and ask them to make sure I was not misunderstanding him.

The nurse said, "No, you did not misunderstand, the radiologist came by, but you were not in the room, so he told Clint the news. The angiogram confirmed that the AVM was completely gone, they got it all with the surgery."

Back in the room, Clint asked for a soft drink, more specifically Clint asked for a Mr. Pib. He had one the week before surgery, but now he was remembering that and wanted another one. Of course, I went to the vending machine and got him one.

During the day, I would sit right by Clint's bed. I would help him by cutting up his food so he could eat, and we would talk. He was understanding most words, but still struggling to respond with the right words. He would try, and he seemed to know what he was trying to say, but it was as if the signals were getting crossed from his brain to his mouth. Sometimes he would get close to the right word and I would say the right word and he could repeat, but other times the word was so far off I would not understand what he was trying to tell me, and this frustrated the both of us.

We also watched a lot of game shows and The Andy Griffith show, which is one of Clint's all-time favorites. In the afternoon, I would turn the TV to a music channel, and we would listen to music. We did that often.

Once, when we were listening to music, an eighties song came on with a good beat, and I danced in my chair and rhetorically asked Clint if he remembered that song.

He nodded and said clearly, "Yes, Collins."

I looked at him and then realized that it was in fact a song by Phil Collins. I said, "Clint, oh my goodness, that is exactly right! Good for you!"

Later, an occupational therapist came in to evaluate Clint. It was quite an effort, but with help from the nurse to level his drainage tube and the help of another therapist, they were able to get Clint upright and sitting on the side of his bed. Progress. They also used a white board and ask Clint if he could write his name. He did. It was shaky, and looked like a kindergartener had written it, but that was okay—he did it!

I stayed with Clint until after his dinner came. I helped him set up his tray so he could eat. He had had a big day, and I could tell he was tired. I left around 7pm for the drive back to Arab.

The next day when I arrived, they told me they were going to take Clint for another CT scan to check the brain swelling. At this point, they were doing a CT scan every other day. And just like the days past, no change. That was a little discouraging. Dr. Fisher said again that I should just be patient and give it time. Easier said than done.

One cool thing that happened was that they sent in a music therapist. She explained that sometimes when someone is having trouble with the brain connecting to make the correct words, music helps. Singing is directed from a different part of the brain, who knew? But that would explain why there have been people who stutter when they speak, but yet can sing perfectly.

She pulled out her guitar and asked me what kind of music Clint likes. I told her that he likes classic rock. She started playing the Eagles classic, *Take it Easy*. When she hit the chorus, Clint belted out the words too. He was out of tune and out of pitch, but he sang with her word for word. That was music to my ears. She told him how good he had done. She then went into her bag and pulled out some Maracas. She put one into Clint's left hand, the hand that he had not been able to use at all since surgery. She told him that when she played the guitar, she wanted him to sing again, but also to play along with the maracas, if he was able to. She started playing The Steve Miller Band's, *"The Joker."* Clint again sang out at the chorus. Then I looked down at his left hand. It was very slowly moving the maracas. I started to cry with joy. It was one of the coolest, most miraculous things I had ever seen.

Clint was still struggling to speak but was communicating better for sure. Mostly, conveying his aggravation, he did not like the thickening agent in his drinks; he did not like all the medicine, the disruptions during the night. He was homesick. We all craved normalcy, I got that. And while I hated that he was uncomfortable, I thought the fact he was continuing to complain more and more was a good thing.

CHAPTER 23

D
r. Fisher told me they planned to clamp Clint's drainage tube. He was hoping that the brain swelling would have gone down by now. As he explained to me, if you sprain your wrist and it swells, the soft tissue allows for it to do so without any complications, but with the brain, because the skull is rigid and enclosed, there is not much room for swelling. He said that the brain is composed of the brain itself, which is surrounded by Cerebrospinal fluid (CSF). The body produces and disposes of the fluid around the brain on its own. But when there is swelling of the brain, it displaces the fluid against the skull causing pressure on the brain. With Clint's AVM and subsequent surgery, the brain was swollen and that was blocking the body's ability to drain the CSF that it was producing.

Normally as the healing process continues, the swelling goes down and the body resumes doing what it is supposed to do, including disposing of the extra CSF fluid. That is amazing, isn't it? But Clint was eight days post op., and the swelling was just not going down as quickly as hoped.

Dr. Fisher explained that over time, with a tube inserted into the brain to drain fluid externally, there was a risk of germs and infection. The drainage tube is a great option, but only short term. So, he told me they were going to clamp the CSF tube during the night to see if Clint's body could respond and do what it was supposed to do. If it did so for at least twenty-four hours, they could take the tube out and get Clint out of ICU.

But once the drain was clamped, if the fluid started building up again and putting pressure on the brain again, Dr. Fisher said he would have to consider putting in a shunt, a permanent internal drainage tube inserted into the brain. The tubing then passes under the skin into the abdomen.

The next morning when I came in, they had, in fact, clamped the EVD (drain) during the night, and it did not go well. Dr. Fisher told me that Clint would be going back in for surgery the following day to insert the shunt. I was dismayed. I asked, "Could we please just give it a little more time?" He said that we could but, in his opinion, as there would not be enough time to make a difference. The swelling was just not coming down quickly enough and the longer the drain stayed in, the more the increase of infection. He assured me that the shunt procedure was a relatively common and safe procedure.

The shunt would become permanent, the tissue would heal around it and there would be no need risking another surgery to remove it. I was disappointed at the news, but it did make sense. The surgery was scheduled for Thursday, which happened to be the same day that I was scheduled to meet with my surgeon because of the diverticulitis. Travis was supposed to spend the day with Clint.

I called Travis and told him what was going on. He told me to keep my appointment and not to worry that he would be there for Clint's procedure. I was torn, but he assured me that he would update me all along the way.

On Thursday, Travis and his wife, Juanita, arrived in Birmingham at 6am. Clint was scheduled for surgery at 7. Just as he promised, he started texting me from the moment they arrived.

My doctor's appointment was at 11am. At this point, I had been battling Diverticulitis for almost two months. When the doctor came in, I started crying. *Geez, why do I cry so much lately?* She and her nurse asked me why I was crying, and I just started babbling, "Because I know that you are going to want me to have surgery, and while I want to feel better, my son is in the hospital in Birmingham having surgery right now as we speak, and I can't have surgery right now. I just can't."

The doctor told me that she wanted to first look at the CT scans they ran at the hospital to figure out what was going on. When she came back into the room, she confirmed that each of the scans showed that the infection was in the same place. But, in each subsequent scan, the infection appeared not to be as severe as in the one before. She thought that the medicines they had given me were just not the right ones and therefore, were not completely knocking out the infection. She said that she did not want to do surgery, she just wanted to change my medicine instead, and see me back again in a month.

I said, "So I don't have to have surgery? The ER doctor told me that I probably would have to for sure."

"No, not at this time."

The relief and all the stress caught up with to me, I think, so that I could not stop crying. And then an amazing thing happened. The nurse looked at me and said, "I see that you wear a cross around your neck. Are you a Christian?"

I said, "Yes, I am."

"Would it be okay if we prayed with you?"

I was a little surprised, but I said, "Absolutely, Thank you."

Right then she and the surgeon both dropped to their knees and held my hands and prayed for my health and prayed for Clint. It was moving and it was powerful. When they finished, they stood up and both hugged me.

A short time later, I received a text from Travis that Clint's surgery was over. He was in recovery and had done fine. Everything went well. Travis told me that he and Juanita would not leave his side.

I went home. It was the first time I had been at my house during the day in over two weeks. Jessica was an officer for her high school's Health Occupations Students of America club (HOSA). It was the night of the homecoming parade. She was riding in the parade in a convertible. She was a senior, and it was her last homecoming parade, and I was going to be able to be there. It then dawned on me how little I had been there for Jessica in weeks. She never complained, but I still felt bad. I went to the parade and then came home and she and Matt and I had dinner together. I felt normal again for a moment, and refreshed, ready to face the hospital the following morning.

In the meantime, Travis kept his word. He texted and updated me every hour or two. I was grateful. Travis and I had not always gotten along, but to credit where due, he was phenomenal. He texted me at around 8pm to tell me that without the EVD drain in anymore, they were moving Clint out of ICU and into a room. Clint was very sore but was sitting up and eating. Travis and Juanita stayed with him until well after 10pm.

I went to bed with a light heart, thankful that Clint's surgery went well, thankful to Travis and Juanita, thankful that I did not have to have surgery, especially now, and thankful to be there for Jessica. I could not wait to get back to Birmingham. Clint was in a room, hallelujah!

CHAPTER 24

The next day, I was on the road by six am and arrived in Birmingham by eight. Clint was awake when I walked into his new room. He smiled widely.

Clint's room was a typical hospital room, but when I walked in and saw it, I felt like he and I had won the jackpot. There was a bathroom and a couch/bench, which would be my bed, a recliner, and a television. It was so wonderful to be out of ICU.

For the surgery, they had to go back into the incision in Clint's skull to place the shunt. And in order to get it properly positioned in his stomach, they also had to do a laparoscopic incision into his belly. He was very sore. His color was good though. The nurse came in and suggested that he try to spend some time in the recliner. She said the more he could stay out of the bed, the better for his recovery. I agreed and she and I worked together to get him up and into the chair to eat breakfast. He and I watched an episode of *Andy Griffith*. Then he was ready to lie back down. He was not up for long, but it was a start.

His speech was still not good. His vocabulary had increased, but some words escaped him, while others would still come out completely wrong.

Back during the eighties, the television show, *Saturday Night Live*, had a skit with entertainers, Joe Piscopo and Robin Duke, called *Doug and Wendy Whiner*. For years, if someone in our family started whining about anything, it was an inside joke to quote one of the lines from their skit, which was, "We're Doug and Wendy Whiner, we can't eat that because we have diverticulitis…"

I had been at the hospital with Clint for a couple of hours when it occurred to him that I had not been there the day before. He kept trying to ask me something, but I was struggling to understand. He kept saying, "Mom your," followed by some sound that made absolutely no sense. He got very frustrated with me.

I told him, "Clint, I am sorry. I am trying, but I don't know what you are trying to say."

After going on with this for a few minutes, he blurted out clearly, "Mom, you know, Doug and Wendy Whiner!"

I cracked up and said, "You mean my diverticulitis?"

"Yeah…"

He then smiled, relieved that I finally understood.

I cannot describe how amazing this encounter was for me, for one thing, with everything going on, Clint remembered that I may need surgery and was worried about me, but also, he figured out a complex way to convey what he was trying to say when the words had escaped him, and without meaning to, Clint had said something hilarious once again. It just signified such hope. I knew that somewhere deep down my Clint was still in there.

A bit later, there was a knock at the door. It was staff members from the rehab center coming in to evaluate Clint. They came in with a walker and a wheelchair. They did a physical assessment of Clint and then announced that they were going to try to get him up and walking. They put a belt around his waist so that they could hold on to him with it. The two of them got him up and to the walker. One followed behind him, holding on to him the entire time. The other walked behind with the wheelchair. They started down the hall, with the aid of the walker Clint was able to walk about five or six feet down the hall, before he needed to use the wheelchair to be wheeled back to the room. Five or six feet may not seem like a lot, but it was monumental; it was the first time Clint had walked since before surgery, eleven days before. When he got back in the room, he was completely worn out, but he did it!

They told me that they would be transferring Clint into inpatient rehabilitation within the next few days. Matt and I surmised that would happen on Monday after the weekend.

I spent the night on the couch in Clint's room. When we awoke the following morning, they once again had Clint up in the chair and up to walk a few feet. Travis and Juanita came back to visit. While they were there, we asked the nurses if we could use the wheelchair to take Clint out of the room. It wound up being quite an ordeal, even though we were in a hospital, we had a hard time finding a wheelchair to use. We also needed a covering for Clint's head, his hair was shaven, and he had staples going all the way from top to bottom. I did not want him to get stared at and feel self-conscious. It took hours just to get the wheelchair and head covering. Things at the hospital move slowly. However, we finally got it. Travis, Juanita, and I wheeled Clint down the hall onto the elevator, and outside the front door. We sat outside the hospital in the fresh air for about ten minutes until Clint was tired again. But it was good for his morale and ours, too. It was the first time that Clint had been outside in almost two weeks.

Right before Travis and Juanita left, my cousin's wife, Michelle, and her son, Paul, came in. For the rest of the day, Clint rested while we talked. They left mid-afternoon. I stayed with Clint until after dinner and then went home for the evening.

The next day was Sunday. I stayed home and Matt came to the hospital to spend the day with Clint. He had not been there since the week before. He wanted to see Clint and he also wanted to give me a break from the hospital. So, he went to Birmingham, and I went to the Funky Feather. I was so grateful for my manager and staff because it was the first time I had been at my own business in weeks and yet everything had run smoothly.

In the middle of the afternoon, Matt called me and told me that they were moving Clint to the Spain Rehabilitation Center.

I said, "Today? But it is Sunday."

"Yes, but they have a room available; they want to get him settled in tonight and start therapy first thing in the morning."

CHAPTER 25

S pain Rehabilitation appeared to be a repurposed old hospital from the 1960's. The whole facility had the smell of an old building, with square tiles on the walls of the long corridors and incredibly old elevators. The staff was very capable, no doubt, but the building itself seemed a little creepy.

Clint's room was huge. It had been a semi-private room with two of everything at one time but had been converted into a single occupancy room. There was the same couch/bench in the room that had been in his room at the hospital. There was also a recliner. Clint was assigned his own wheelchair. We were told that we should consider ourselves no longer in the "hospital," and even though there were doctors and nurses at the rehab center, they would be as least intrusive as possible, only coming in for rounds, to administer medicine, or if needed. Beyond that, the therapist would be taking care of Clint while we were there. We were also told that we could go anywhere within the center or outside that we wanted, so long as we did not leave the premises. There was a quaint little sitting area outside with trees and benches. We spent a lot of time there. There were vending machines in the basement and a family game/tv room down the hall. Clint would be receiving four hours of therapy every day, including physical, occupational, and speech. Each step of Clint's journey was less restrictive. He went from the ICU to a hospital room, and now to rehab. And each one lead us one step closer to home.

On Monday, Clint's first day of therapy, I got up early and went to Birmingham. His therapy began at eight o'clock sharp with occupational therapy. His therapist's name was Amelia. She was young, maybe in her twenties, newly out of college and working her internship. She was sweet, but also focused and efficient. Amelia's first task started with getting Clint into a shower. He had a shower chair. She taught me how to safely get him out of his wheelchair and in and out of the shower. After the shower, Amelia helped Clint dress and wheeled him to the sink. She then worked with him for another fifteen minutes to brush his teeth. She assisted a little, but mostly made him learn how to do it again for himself. Next was putting on shoes and learning to tie them again. He struggled a lot with that task. It takes a lot of dexterity to tie shoes.

After close to a half hour, he was ready. She then wheeled him down to the second floor. The floor was divided into two gyms. One was for work with occupational therapy tasks, the other was a physical therapy gym, there was a long corridor separating the two.

The purpose of occupational therapy was to relearn life and work skills, things that deal with dexterity, such as how to use kitchen appliances, personal hygiene, the things you would need to do in just the basic course of living day to day life. Amelia would constantly evaluate and figure out modifications to different skills when he struggled. Like for instance, when she realized how much Clint had struggled to tie his shoes, she got him non-tie laces, laces made of elastic that made Clint's shoes more like slip-ons. In the Occupational gym, there were puzzles, walking bars, a kitchen, and all kinds of varied skill testing things to work on.

Physical Therapy dealt more with building up physical strength, and helped with balance, depth perception, walking, and climbing stairs. Modifications could also be made there, too, if needed, such as continued use of a wheelchair, or use of a cane, just for an example. The purpose of both therapies was to work with Clint to reteach him everything he could learn, to achieve the baseline of the things he could do prior to surgery, and to be independent, and secondarily to modify when needed.

Clint also had speech therapy every day. There they worked on retraining the neurons in the brain to connect in the right way. He had to learn how to say a lot of words all over again, in this area of therapy, they also worked with teaching Clint how to read and write again too.

Clint's days at rehab were grueling. A typical day started at eight and would include an hour of occupational therapy, an hour of physical therapy, a half hour of speech therapy. We would then have about an hour break until lunch. We would eat lunch and then at 1:00 pm, they would come back and get him and there would be another half hour of occupational, physical, and speech therapy, for a total of four hours every day. Therapy ended at 3:30 and then dinner came in at five. That was the basics of the everyday schedule, but there were also opportunities for Clint to get a shave or a haircut, there were educational classes dealing with life after a head injury, and there was still occasional music therapy. There were also medical checkups, every morning the doctor made his rounds and in the evening the nurses were in to give Clint his medicine. After dinner, the rest of the night was free time for Clint. The side effect of the medicine Clint was taking, and the therapy was that he was usually worn out and ready to go to bed by eight thirty or nine.

Most nights, I stayed with Clint especially since the nurses were not in as often as they were in the hospital. I did not like leaving him there alone, especially since he could not walk without help. I was torn though for many reasons, the first being Matt and Jessica, I felt like I was letting them down, but also, honestly, when I was at the rehab with him, I just did not sleep well on the bench in his room. I finally settled on a routine of staying every other night and driving back and forth on the other. On the nights I stayed, I would get up and help him to the restroom, set my clock in the morning to help him with breakfast and to help him get dressed and ready for therapy. On the nights that I came home, I was almost neurotic communicating with the night nurses about coming in more often to check on him and help him. I would make sure the nurse on duty knew my phone number and I would drill Clint on how to use the call button and remind him that he should not get out of the bed on his own without help. I worried the whole time that I was away. In fairness though, I must say the staff at the rehab center were great. They were helpful, professional, and dedicated.

On Clint's first day of therapy, after finishing with Amelia, he was turned over to Ingrid and Liz—they were his physical therapy team. On the first day, Ingrid told him that they were going to work on walking. She put a cloth belt around his waist so that she could hold on to him and they took off down the hall. Clint looked down at his feet the entire time. His pace was slow, and he tottered as if he had been drinking. I could tell by watching him that he was weak and unsure of himself and of his balance. He was extremely cautious with every step. Ingrid and he walked down the corridor between the gyms. They had just walked about thirty feet when Clint announced that he was tired. She grabbed a chair and he sat for about ten minutes. She then asked if he thought he could make it back to his wheelchair, which was still in the gym. He said he could, and they walked back in the same manner.

His speech therapist was named Charlotte. She was like a cheerleader, spunky, charismatic, and encouraging. She worked with Clint to relearn language. He could talk, but many times the brain would misfire and send the wrong signals, and words would fail him. That was always frustrating, because he knew what he wanted to say but could not always get it out. Other times, the words would come out, but not exactly right, especially compound words or complex sentences. Charlotte would say words and have Clint repeat them. She used a series of proven tests, lesson plans, and goals that she patiently worked through daily: as he mastered one, she would move to something more difficult. It was fascinating to watch and reminded me of someone teaching a small child to read and learn vocabulary. I guess it was basically the same thing. She would use flash cards, pictures, and repetition. If he got something right, she would cheer, brag, give him a high fives. Clint responded to that type of praise well, it seemed to encourage him to continue the work.

Being at the rehab center with Clint was humbling, not only by seeing Clint work so hard, but also witnessing other patients that were in the gym at the same time. Some of them were far worse off than Clint. Some, I found out, had been living at the rehab center for months. They all were working hard to get better. I was inspired.

The therapists pushed Clint. It was amazing to see the progress from day to day and the staff's dedication. After we had been there for several days, Amelia asked Clint if there was something specifically that he wanted to work on. She asked him to tell her somethings he did when he was home. He named three things he wanted to practice: bagging groceries for his job at WDG, feeding the dogs, and loading the dishwasher. I will never forget how she took Clint into the kitchen at the rehab center and took all the food out of the cabinets, found some bags, and simulated with him bagging groceries at work. She then used small blocks in a bucket as pretend dog food, gave him a scoop and some bowls, and worked with him on filling the bowls and safely putting them on the floor without falling, she did it several times.

The next day, Travis came to Birmingham and stayed with Clint, so I could be at home for Jessica's last pep rally and Band Senior Night. Amelia continued where she left off. She then suggested they do something fun;

her suggestion was for her and Clint to make cookies. They did that and when they finished, Amelia worked with Clint to do the dishes and load the dishwasher.

In physical therapy, Liz also challenged Clint more each day. She would make him walk further and further, she added hills, uneven pavement, and then stairs. One day she even took him into the parking lot and taught him how to balance himself while getting in and out of a car. She was trying to work with him in real life situations.

They also taught me, things such as how to hold on to Clint's belt to make sure he did not fall at home, how to balance myself to help him navigate stairs, how to get him in and out of the shower safely.

Clint spent nine work-filled days at Spain Rehab. On October 29, he was finally released to go home. He would continue outpatient therapy at a rehab center close to our house. He had been in the hospital for twenty-five days during this stay, and a total of thirty-four days within the past two months. He still had a lot of work and recovery to do. But we were excited. We were going home!

CHAPTER 26

I cannot describe how excited we were to be on the way back from Birmingham with Clint in the car with us. Clint's speech was much better, he was able to communicate. Occasionally he would still mispronounce a word, but with correction, he could say it right. The mild corrections went on for a couple of months, but overall, he was back to himself with speech. He could read and he could write, although for a while, I will admit his handwriting looked like that of a five-year-old. But honestly, that was okay, we could work on that. I was just thankful that he still had that ability.

Walking on a flat surface was fine; he had mastered that. He still walked cautiously but had come so far. So, within the house, he could safely go from room to room by himself. However, maneuvering stairs and uneven ground was still a struggle. I was taught how to use the belt around his waist to help him whenever we had to leave the house.

Matt and I bought some baby monitors and put one in Clint's room and one in ours, so that when we were asleep, we could hear him if he got up. I found that I was overly protective of Clint.

When we got home, Clint was taking sixteen different pills a day. Some of those were steroids. We once again were instructed to wean him off of those. Because of the steroids, Clint had a lot of puffiness and weight gain, especially in his face. We were told that was common. And as he came off them, he did eventually lose the excess weight. He was also taking two different anti-seizure medicines, this was also common after having such a major brain surgery, But Dr. Fisher wanted us to try and slowly wean him off one of those as well. His hair also started growing back. He was starting to physically look like himself again.

We also started outpatient rehabilitation at the hospital close to our house. Clint's therapist there was named Scott, and he saw Clint for an hour, three days a week, for almost two months. As each day and therapy went by, you could see vast improvement. At the same time, Clint's brain was continuing to heal also, which, I am sure, had something to do with the improvements as well.

Matt, Jessica, and I worked it out so that one of us could be home with Clint always. By working together, it gave me some flexibility to do what I needed to do at The Funky Feather or with grocery shopping and errands.

Being back at the Funky Feather rejuvenated my soul. Not only was I grateful to my staff for all that they had done while I was out to keep everything going, I also received so much love from the community. I could have never imagined how many customers would tell me that they were praying for our family and for Clint. Strangers and friends alike also told me that Clint's name was added to their prayer list at their church. That was certainly humbling, but also a reminder of God's faithfulness. I fully believe that their prayers and outpouring of love made a difference.

In the beginning of November, Matt's brother, Bobby, called. He and his wife, Susie, still lived in the town in Michigan where Matt grew up. Matt's eighty-six-year-old dad did, as well. Bobby said that he and Susie were heading out west to spend the holidays with their son and his family. He told Matt that their dad (Papa) wanted to come and spend time with us while they were away. We were excited. Matt's dad was a veteran, he was also a retired policeman and a retired preacher. He was always such a kind man.

Matt and I went out and bought a twin-size bed and borrowed a folding screen, we moved our kitchen table out and made walls out of the screens and carved out a little impromptu bedroom for papa in the breakfast nook area adjacent to the kitchen. It was different, but it worked.

Bobby and Matt planned to meet in Indiana to exchange Papa. I stayed behind with Clint and Jessica. Jessica and I cleaned house and I made a roast on the day of his arrival. For a couple of days, it was genuinely nice having Papa with us. But as each day followed, he seemed to be more and more out of sorts. He was getting confused with details, he reminisced about things going way back, such as the time with his high school girlfriend and of his time serving in the Korean War. At other times, things seemed normal and then he would switch and be almost hostile towards Matt or me. It was confusing.

We spent Thanksgiving with all our children and grandchildren and Papa. It was a wonderful time. But shortly afterwards, papa announced that he wanted to go back to Michigan. He said he made a mistake coming because God had a mission for him back home. When we ask what kind of mission, he said he would only know when he got back there. We reminded him that he was supposed to stay with us through Christmas, which was in three weeks. We promised him that after Christmas, we would take him back to Michigan. He told us that three weeks was way too long to wait, he needed to go back sooner because God had told him to.

Matt called Bobby and told him what was going on and Bobby said that when he left his son's house in a couple of days, he would drive to Alabama and pick Papa up and take him back to Michigan with him. And that is what he did.

As December rolled around, we finally finished weaning Clint's off one of his anti-seizure medicines. He was taking very little medicine compared to when he first came home. Matt and I noticed that his thought processes seemed to be clicking better, his speech was almost back to normal, but more importantly, he seemed to be understanding things better as well, maybe even better than he did before surgery. We wondered aloud if some of the cognitive disabilities he had endured for his entire life may get better too. We also started seeing Clint's funny personality reemerge.

One day he walked out to the sunporch where Matt and I were sitting and announced that he heard that they were making a sequel to the movie Titanic, "Titanic Two," he said.

I retorted, "Clint, that seems kid of dumb to me, how can they do that when in the end of the first one, the boat sank, and everyone died."

"Mom, obviously, it will not be the same actors!"

Around the same time, Jessica had a saxophone solo in her high school band's Christmas Spectacular show, we were able to take Clint, and all go as a family to see her. In December, Clint also finished his last therapy session. Things were going well.

On December 10, 2019, we took Clint back to Birmingham for his first post operation follow up. When we arrived, Clint spotted Dr. Fisher in the hallway and just walked right up to him and smiled big. Dr. Fisher immediately greeted Clint with a huge smile, and a firm handshake, and said joyfully, "Hey, look who's here; it's my man, Clint!"

The interaction made me happy. Dr. Fisher is one of the most prominent neurosurgeons in the country. Yet, I realized that Clint does not understand that concept, the one of pretense or importance; he is not impressed or intimidated by a title. He just knows when he likes someone and always seems to sense when they sincerely like him back, which Dr. Fisher seemed to do. I do not know why it touched me so, but I realized that somewhere along this journey Clint had decided that Dr. Fisher was his friend.

When Dr. Fisher came into Clint's room, he said that his CT scan looked "amazing." He told us that the swelling from the AVM and surgery had gone down quite a bit and everything appeared to be healing great! I just thanked Jesus for so many answered prayers.

Dr. Fisher lifted Clint's restrictions, and told us that Clint could go back to work and start doing things on his own again. He said, "It is time to get back to normal."

We made another appointment for six months. As we left, Clint asked me, "Mom, I know that Dr. Fisher said I could go back to work, but do you think it would be okay if I wait until the first of the year?"

"Yes, I suppose that would be okay, but why? I know how much you want to be back there."

He continued, "I know, but I don't think I am quite ready yet. I think I will be in a couple of weeks, though."

"If that is how you feel, I think that will be just fine."

"Will Miss Cindy be mad at me?"

"I don't think that she will. I will just let her know that you can return back to work after the New Year. I think that will be okay."

He said, "I sure hope that you are right. I really don't want her to be mad or disappointed with me. I think I will be ready in a couple of weeks."

That was the first time I had ever seen that in Clint, a nervousness about resuming his life. He had come to rely on me as a safety net. I realized in the next couple of weeks we needed to build his confidence back up and reinforce the thought within him that he could do it.

When Christmas came, Matt and I were blessed to have all our children, grandchildren, Matt's sister and brother-in-law, and nephew join us for the day. As I looked around the room and listened to the opening of presents and the laughter, I just felt love. It was such a great day.

CHAPTER 27

January 3, 2020, I awoke at 6:30am and went into the kitchen to make coffee. Clint came out of his room and joined me. I looked at him and realized that he was in his work uniform. He had already showered, dressed, had his shoes on, and was ready to go.

I said, "Well Clint, today is the day that you go back to work. Are you excited?"

"Yes."

"I see that you are already ready."

"Yep."

I paused before continuing, "Clint, you do know that you don't have to be there until twelve, right?"

"Yeah, I know, but I don't want to be late."

Somethings never change. I did not laugh in front of him. I just poured my coffee and went about starting my morning, but inside I felt real joy. We had come full circle. Clint was going back to work at the grocery store, where he had been employed at for almost eleven years. He had not been there since August. And now here he was standing before me, excited, and ready five and a half hours before he was supposed to be there.

Clint's first day back was great. When he came home, he went straight to bed for a nap. He had never done that before, yet as he continued to work, that became the new normal for him. He just did not have the same stamina as before surgery. Much of that was caused by the anti-seizure medicines that he was on, which also made him tired. Since we were weaning him down to a smaller dose, I assumed that would get better in time.

Matt and I were able to get back to a fully normal schedule at the Funky Feather again. That felt good. It was the start of our fourth year in business, sales were good. In fact, the business was having the best sales month it had since we opened. We felt hopeful and optimistic.

Late in January, Bobby called Matt to let him know that Papa had fallen. When they got him to the hospital to make sure he was okay, they discovered that he had a brain tumor and was also in the onset of dementia. The tumor was inoperable, and Papa did not want to go through any treatments. The news was not good. The doctor told Bobby that there was no way Papa could live alone. He suggested a nursing home with staffers that could give him around-the-clock care. I felt so bad for Matt. He was heartbroken.

And it was then that his dad's behavior in November was finally understood, too. Matt wished he had realized what was happening when he was here. It was a sad realization. After Papa was released from the hospital, he was moved into his new place in the nursing home in Michigan.

On Clint's third Friday back to work, I pulled into the parking lot to pick him up at the end of his shift. I parked at the front of the store. I had been sitting there for a few minutes when a couple of employees from the grocery store came running out and motioning to me. I got out of the car and one of them said, "Are you Clint's mom?"

"Yes."

"Come quick, something is wrong; he is crying and needs you to come in."

I proceeded quickly into the store while trying to process what they had said, why would Clint be crying, and why didn't he just come out to the car? I was confused. As I walked through the door, Cindy yelled out to me, "Come quicker! Clint is having a seizure."

I ran over to him. Clint was right in the front of the entire grocery store, laid over at his waist on the end of one of the checkout counters. His feet were on the floor and the side of his face was lying on the counter, his arms weirdly contorted by his side. He was in a full blown grand mal seizure, another first for him.

I lay over the counter beside him, completely oblivious of where I was, who was there, or what else was going on. Right then and there, it was just me and him in the world. I was rubbing his back and talking incessantly to him, "I am here, Clint… you are okay… I am here… I got you, buddy… you're okay."

I was scared to death. My brain prayed: "My God, please let him be okay."

Clint seized for about two or three minutes. When he came out of it, he was disorientated. He awoke to his coworkers and customers all looking on, yet he had no idea what had just happened. Cindy brought over a chair, some water, and a cold towel. As he sat there and drank the water, he slowly came back to himself. It dawned on me that he had never had a seizure like that before and he was only three months post op, his brain was still healing. This could be something serious. I said to Cindy, "Will you please call the paramedics?"

She did so and within about five minutes they arrived with their lights and sirens blaring. If we had not been the center of attention already, we most certainly were now. I told the paramedics what had happened previously with his surgery and expressed that I just wanted him checked out to make sure there was nothing more serious going on. They checked his vitals, and everything seemed okay. The paramedic told me they could transport him to the hospital, but they really thought that he was okay to go home and just rest. Clint had come to his senses. But the seizure had left him feeling weak and exhausted. I helped him out to the car, and we headed home.

Once we got home, I decided that I should try and get in touch with Dr. Fisher's office, just in case. It was after-hours, so I was not able to reach him, but I did speak to a nurse manning the phone service. She asked a lot of detailed questions, and then told me that she thought I should take him somewhere and have him checked out. She said I could just take him to the local hospital. So that was what I did.

The emergency room doctor listened to me intently. He asked a lot of questions about the surgery and took that seriously. I was grateful. He ordered a CT scan. Everything seemed okay. He could tell that the brain was clearly still healing. He felt that the seizure was just a one off caused by the healing process. He said he would send the CT scan report to Dr. Fisher and wanted me to follow up with him on Monday.

Once we got back home, Clint looked at me with a serious look on his face and asked, "Mom, why did I have a seizure."

"Because the brain is still healing. It just kind of misfired, that's all, but I think you are still doing okay."

He continued, "You know what I hate, Mom? I hate that it happened to me while I was at work in front of everybody. They were all staring at me and now they are going to think I am not like them; they are going to think something is wrong with me."

He broke my heart. I said, "No, baby, they aren't going to think differently of you. They were just worried about you. That's all."

"I don't think so; I think they are going to think I am weird."

I said, "Clint, would you think that about one of your friends if it happened to them? Would you think they were weird?"

"No."

"Well, okay then. It will be okay, I promise."

On the following Monday, I spoke to someone in Dr. Fisher's office. They told me that he had looked at the CT scan and felt the same as the ER doctor that the seizure was just a brain misfire in the healing process, but he also felt that it could have been because we were premature in weaning Clint off some of his anti-seizure medicines. He told me that he was going to put him back on the dose that he was on when he came home from the hospital. He thought that it would be for the best for a while, an opportunity to give Clint's brain more healing time. That was okay, except the medicine really did make Clint so tired and a little lethargic. It was only a small setback, but a setback all the same. They told me not to get discouraged. They said that, with brain surgery, it can take at least a year for the brain to heal completely and sometimes it even takes longer. They reassured me that Clint was doing well, considering it had only been three months post surgery.

We did not let that setback stop us for long. Clint took the next weekend off and then right back to work. On his first day back, I could tell that he was nervous. I was a little nervous, too; I did not want him to have another seizure, especially while at work. But I did not want him to know that I was worried. I encouraged him and reminded him that we can never know what will happen from day to day, but we must live our lives. This seemed to sink in. And he did fine.

CHAPTER 28

Jessica was a Senior in High School. She decided that upon her graduation she wanted to pursue a career in nursing. She credited my mom and her nurses as her inspiration. In February, she told us that her HOSA club would be assisting the Special Education class for a couple of upcoming events. She told us that she had volunteered to be a buddy coach for an athlete in the Special Olympics and she would also be escorting a student to "A Night to Shine," a prom for disabled students and adults. I cannot tell you how proud I was of her.

The Funky Feather was still doing well, in fact it was exceeding the previous year's sales. Everything seemed to be headed in the right direction.

On March 12, 2020, Jessica left for Orlando, Florida, with the high school band. They were invited to march in a parade at Disney World. It was such an exciting time. They left on Thursday and planned to return on the following Tuesday.

Monday the 16th was Clint's thirtieth birthday. I could not help but think about what the doctor told us when they found the AVM… "Many times, when they find an AVM, it is during autopsy, after a brain-bleed, which typically occurs between the age of thirty to thirty-five." It hit me hard, Clint was turning thirty, the AVM was gone, and we were celebrating! Thank you, Jesus.

On Friday, one day after the band arrived in Orlando, we found out that Jessica would be returning home early. They were told that they could march in the parade on Saturday night as planned, but then would be coming home first thing Sunday morning. There was COVID viral pandemic making its way through the country and President Trump had announced that the government would be shutting everything down for a couple of weeks to "stop the spread". The band was instructed by the superintendent that they had to come home early. We had no idea the impact this virus would have on us all.

The Funky Feather, along with every other "non-essential' business was shut down. We could operate the restaurant for curbside pick-up only. But all the other aspects of my business were shut down, the birthday parties already booked were canceled and laser tag and the arcade were closed. We were operating at about twenty percent of our normal gross sales. I had to lay off eight of my employees. That part was the most devasting.

Fortunately, we had many loyal customers who ordered curbside pick-up from us every single week. We had customers who gave us donations or bought gift cards that I doubt they ever used. All of this was an effort to sustain us during the lockdown. I was truly humbled. I was also more determined than ever to try to weather the storm.

The two-week lockdown wound up lasting for over two months in Alabama, longer than that in many other states. And when we finally could reopen, it was only at fifty percent capacity. That is a difficult position for any restaurant running on small margins to begin with. We wondered if there was a way to make it work or if we would even be able to pay the bills. I told Matt, "In the past four years, we have worked so hard to grow our business. I do not want this to be what brings us down."

One afternoon near the beginning of the lockdown, Jessica stormed out of her room, crying. I asked, "What's wrong?"

"They just announced that they are closing school for the rest of the year."

It was two months before her graduation. That was so personally devastating, her senior year, and it ended before prom, before awards day, before all the fun year-end events that all the seniors work so hard for and look forward to. It was sudden; she was saddened that she may never be able to tell her classmates and her teachers goodbye. She was aware that she may not see many of those people ever again, yet there was no closure, no chance to end this chapter properly before moving on to the next.

And while she and I both realized that, in the grand scheme of things, what she was going through was small compared to others, but in that moment, it did not make her loss seem any less sad. Jessica's class was born in the year of 9/11 and was set to graduate in the year of a historical pandemic. I must believe that she and her peers will be the generation to make a difference one day. They have lived history. For Jessica, these historical events were just the bookends to all the other adversities she had faced in the middle.

At the end of March, my uncle, Quitman, my dad's last living brother, died. He had been battling cancer for a couple of years, his death came suddenly though. One week he seemed to be doing well, and the next he was gone. And because we were in the middle of a pandemic, we were unable to have a funeral.

And in Michigan, the nursing homes were all shut down to families. Matt's dad had just gone into a nursing home one month before and now was alone and not allowed visitors.

The whole situation was heartbreaking all the way around.

CHAPTER 29

By the Summer of 2020, collectively, we were all tired of the "new normal" and all things pandemic: social distancing, masks, and the limited opening of businesses. I think everyone in the entire country was ready for it to be over, but we also learned to function within the new parameters.

The Funky Feather was no exception. We adjusted and adapted by continuing curbside and by partnering with a new food delivery service in town. We were doing better with sales than we had before the pandemic, even with less hours and less capacity. It made no sense really, except that it was just more answered prayers.

Jessica's high school also adapted and figured out a way to give the kids their commencement ceremony. It did not replace all that was lost, but at least it was the closure she needed. At the end of May, we proudly watched as Jessica walked on stage to receive her high school honors diploma. She was also accepted into the honors program at The University of North Alabama.

In the beginning of June, Matt and I took a mini vacation to Biloxi, Mississippi. Clint asked his dad if he could stay with him while we were away. This was a huge step. It was the first time in over ten years that Clint wanted to spend the night at his dad's house. As much as Travis and I have disagreed throughout the years, Clint's decision to get closer with his dad truly made my heart happy. I miss my dad so much; Jessica misses hers too. Clint is lucky to still have Travis; life is too short to live with grudges or hard feelings. And I must admit that Travis has changed throughout the years too; I believe so. He has mellowed and become more patient. Clint had a great time. And Matt and I had a couple of days to skip town alone. We had been a couple for over six years, and this was the first time we had ever been on a trip just by ourselves. We considered it our little honeymoon! It was wonderful and reinvigorating.

At the end of June, Clint had another checkup with Dr. Fisher in

Birmingham. This was the eight-month mark since surgery. They did another MRI. Dr. Fisher said that Clint was "almost back to perfect." Well, I could have told him that. He then told Clint, "I think we easily got you another hundred thousand miles!"

They both laughed. Dr. Fisher said he was so pleased with how well Clint was doing that he did not want to see him again for a year. Great news, although Clint seemed a little upset that he would not get to see his friend again for another year.

Clint continued to improve but the best part of his recovery has been that his personality is still the same. He still amuses me with the little things he says, things which we have affectionately labeled "Clint-isms." One day Clint was talking to Matt and said, "I just want you to know, my door is always open for you if you ever want to talk…well, that is unless it is closed." —Clint-ism

And another—one afternoon I was listening to talk radio. Clint came into the room and said to me, "I bet that guy doesn't make much money because he only works three hours a day; he works less time in a day than I do."

"That is true, but he does make a lot of money, in fact he makes millions." I continued, "Clint, he is a celebrity, so, they don't pay him by the hour; they pay him a lot—just because of who he is."

Clint sat silent for a moment, thinking, and then said, "I wish everyone got paid for being who they are." He continued, "Like you, you are a good mom, and you cook, and you take care of everybody. I think they should pay you just for being who you are."—Clint-ism.

That is who Clint is, though. He is sweet and sincere in all that he does. The only long-term effect of surgery that we have noticed is that Clint has a slight limp in his left leg when he walks. He also still has an occasional mild seizure, but we are working to get that resolved, and he tires more easily. Other than these, Clint is back to himself or maybe even better than he was before surgery. God is good and faithful all the time.

I am optimistic for both Clint and Jessica's future. They have been through so much. Some of their journeys paralleled, but much of their struggles were individually their own. I wish they both could understand how special they are. I wish they could see themselves the way I see them. But they are both a little uncertain and insecure at times. Honestly, I feel the same way. I often wonder if there were things I could have or should have done differently along the way. I second-guess myself, but I am sure that is true of us all. I do not understand why it is human nature to doubt our well thought out decisions, but we all do it, when, really, what we should do is extend ourselves some grace. I am learning.

Life is always full of lessons and some of them are hard, but all we can do is just keep trying. I hope I have instilled that in Clint and Jessica. Failure does not define us, nor does loss. We are still standing, which is the greatest testament to the fact that we tried, we had determination, and, most importantly, we did not give up.

After Dad, Max and Mom died, I remember how many people said that they could not understand how we got through it. They would say things like, if they had gone through the losses like we had, they would have just given up, and they would tell me how strong they thought we were. It just made me aware that people cannot know what they do not know. I realized that their sentiments were well-intended, but what they did not understand was that we never asked for our circumstances, and we were no stronger than anyone else. We just were given no choice. It did not mean that it was not hard. There were times that I wanted to quit, but I also knew that I had to keep going because my children were counting on me. We just had to get through it somehow.

My initial goal for writing this book was to tell Clint's story, because he is one the most courageous and inspirational people I know. I wanted to share his journey in the hope of inspiring others, but as I started writing, I knew that it would be impossible for me to tell his story without also telling mine, Jessica's, my parents', Max's, and Matt's, too. Our struggles and triumphs all intersected, and each journey affected me deeply. I experienced great loss, there is no doubt. But I also experienced great love, and because of that, I feel that I have been incredibly blessed.

Jessica's tenacity to overcome so much loss and at such a young age and yet to excel with such grace amazes me. She is so smart, so capable, and such a force to be reckoned with. I know she will conquer the world one day.

My dad taught me so much. He was the first man I ever loved. I just wish I had not taken our time together for granted. I would give almost anything to be able to sit and talk to him one more time. I am just thankful that as a Christian, I know I will get to do that again one day.

And then there was my mom, she went through so much, yet she never felt sorry for herself. She was a true giver from her heart. Everyone who met her knew that she was something special. I only aspire to be like her one day.

Max left this world far too soon. After he died, I remember how angry I felt toward him for leaving us—crazy right? I now realize that anger was selfish and was such a waste of time, but it was how I felt at the time. In retrospect, I think the anger was just a defense mechanism to keep despair and defeat from overcoming me. I was afraid and the anger motivated me to keep going. I really did not have the opportunity to grieve properly. Now though, I do feel overwhelming grief and sorrow at the loss of Max, I miss him. I also feel sadness for Jessica. She was cheated from so much time. Max died so young and there was still so much he wanted to do. He never got to see Jessica grow into the woman she is, to see all her accomplishments, to know her heart. But I do know that he would be enormously proud.

And then there is Matt. Matt was truly a godsend to me. He is my best friend, and has been a rock for me, Clint, and Jessica. But the most remarkable thing is he did not have to love us. He could have easily walked away, and I would not have blamed him if he had, because when he met us, our lives were a little broken and chaotic. I am so thankful that he saw past that.

As I reflect over the last decade, I never imagined how much differently my life would look compared to what I had thought it would be. Yet, through it all, I learned much about myself, others, and about life in general. Most importantly, I was reminded that I have no control over what happens, but I serve a mighty God who does. And since I found my way back to my faith in Him, I have had a peace that I cannot describe. I also realized how valuable time is and I make a conscious effort to not take any of it for granted. I learned forgiveness—that was a huge one for me. And lastly, I learned that there are truly angels amongst us. No one can do this life alone. I do not know what we would have done had it not been for family, friends, and so many prayers along the way.

And even though I do not know what happens next, I do know that whatever it is; we will face it head-on and keep going—of that I am certain.

GRIEF

A Poem for My Dad
–Jessica Bullock

I can describe in detail the way the clouds bend,

right before the sky falls.

I remember how the earth stopped spinning on its axis,

the moments after I got the news.

Like when your heart skips a beat, and for just a second

you feel like you're about to die, but then you don't.

That's how I felt that day.

I became acquainted with pain much too young.

And though the grieving stage is behind me,

there's still a hole in my heart for you,

stitched together with the glue stick from my pencil pouch,

like all the homemade Father's Day cards and Christmas ornaments.

After you left, I learned to do things without you.

And though I can now cross the street

without your big hands holding mine,

I still find myself reaching for them as my feet hit the crosswalk.

The memories of you still linger in my mind,

And I wonder what you would think of how I turned out.

Years ago, grief was like a tsunami,

And I was still an amateur swimmer,

desperately clawing to keep my nose above the water.

Paula B. Mecomber

Now though, grief comes in waves,

and I'm tall enough to stand without my head going under.

But I still see you in the changing leaves

that signaled both of our birthdays were approaching,

in the light that glimmers off the pool on a July afternoon,

and in the fire that bubbles in the pit of my stomach

when I am passionate or angry.

There's nothing I wouldn't give to hear I love you,

one more time.

But the I love yous are behind me,

just a picture of the past.

And the smell of your clothes has gradually faded from my mind.

So, I'll hold each wave of grief like a hug,

to ensure that your memory never leaves me.

Because even though it hurts,

I hope you never stop crossing my mind.

Clint 1991

Clint 2016

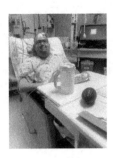

Clint 2019

Jessica and Max 2007

Clint and Jessica 2020

Jessica 2021

Mom & Me 2013

My Dad 2011

Matt and Me 2020

KHARIS PUBLISHING

KHARIS PUBLISHING is an independent, traditional publishing house with a core mission to publish impactful books, and channel proceeds into establishing mini-libraries or resource centers for orphanages in developing countries, so these kids will learn to read, dream, and grow. Every time you purchase a book from Kharis Publishing or partner as an author, you are helping give these kids an amazing opportunity to read, dream, and grow. Kharis Publishing is an imprint of Kharis Media LLC. Learn more at https://www.kharispublishing.com.